"Joined Up Writing This Time Please!"

Stories of Motorsport Heroes

Contents

RAC BRITISH GRAND PRIX 10th JULY 1965
SILVERSTONE
Sponsored by the Daily Express
OFFICIAL PROGRAMME
SUTTON CIRCUIT
COURSE LENGTH 3·2 MILES
SPECTATORS ENCLOSURE
PADDOCK AREA
START
RACE CONTROL
ENTRANCE
PROHIBITED AREA
Autographs
British Empire Trophy Meeting
Organised by B.R.D.C.
OFFICIAL
OULTON PARK
12th APRIL, 1958
For Conditions of Admission see over)
British Racing and Sports Car Club Ltd
MECHANIC
Brands Hatch
August 27 1960
(for conditions of issue see reverse)

Foreword

Martin Tomlinson is one of the elite group of leading full-time motoring artists in Britain. I first met him twenty-five years ago when I organised one of my early motoring and motor racing Art Exhibitions at the Coys Historic Festival at Silverstone. I went on to organise similar exhibitions at Goodwood and more recently for the Royal Automobile Club in Pall Mall and most recently at Sotheby's. Martin was one of my core group, clearly knowledgeable about what he was portraying.

The more I got to know him, the more I realised that he had lived what he was painting. He wasn't just painting Stirling Moss from a faded photograph, he had actually been there, often with his father at trackside and in the paddock. The passion had burned for some sixty years.

One of the problems with exhibitions is that you do a lot of standing or sitting around. The artists chat to a lot of people, many admire or comment on the works and every so often someone buys the painting they will love and cherish for years. Or they might give the artist a commission to paint a specific scene or car. But there is a lot of waiting around.

About a year ago Martin was exhibiting in the Royal Automobile Club in Pall Mall and said to me "I've got something to show you" and produced a slightly dog-eared brown book which I instantly recognised, as I had something very similar. It was, of course, what was often the prized possession of many a schoolboy or girl – an autograph book. The only problem was that mine was mainly filled with autographs of test cricketers and the odd Wolverhampton Wanderers footballer. For the motor racing enthusiast Martin's was altogether different, some of the biggest names of the sport were in there. The first autograph Martin ever obtained, at the age of 8, was Jack Brabham followed by Graham Hill, a good start! Not only that Martin recounted a terrific story of how Hill quickly helped him build his collection. Seven further World Champions later signed the little brown book.

I am not sure if anyone collects autographs any more – I think this very finite connection with the famous and not so famous – probably dwindled about ten years ago. Everyone now just wants a "selfie" with their chosen hero. In America where I still occasionally appear on TV reporting races from the pits, even I get asked to grin at an outstretched arm.

Anyway, Martin and I continued to talk about his fascinating collection and we quickly came to the conclusion – there is a book in this! Martin's paintings and sketches plus my thumbnail biographies of the drivers who had signed. Add in few period photographs, pictures of memorabilia including the programmes Martin had collected. Suddenly we had it – Joined Up Writing This Time Please!

Andrew Marriott

It's in The Blood

My Dad Maurice was born to Charlie and Annie Tomlinson in 1927. Charlie was a practical man, a model maker and an engineer. Annie ran their boarding house in Chester and later on, one in South London. Charlie raced motor bikes in the 1920's and 30's. His dark blue and white, cork crash helmet had 'BMCRC' (British Motor Cycle Racing Club) emblazoned across the front of it and lends credence to this family legend. I also have three Lodge motor cycle spark plugs which have been mounted on a wooden base and carry the legend 'Used at Brooklands BMCRC 1939' in Charlie's handwriting.

Charlie Tomlinson, 344cc Sprint Cotton, 1936

Maurice was taken to race meetings at Brooklands on the pillion of Charlie's various motor bikes. There were also visits to Brands Hatch to watch grass track racing and to Crystal Palace where he saw the likes of Prince Bira, Raymond Mays and Luigi Villoresi. Maurice soon caught the racing bug.

Demobbed after WW2, Maurice got a job with Longmans publishers. The job came with a company car. The first of these was a £671 (including taxes), Standard Vanguard which had a 78.7mph top speed and accelerated from 0-60 in 21.5 secs. Various Morris Oxford models followed.

Sir Malcolm Campbell, 'Bluebird', Brooklands Members banking, 1936

In the 1950's he did some competition driving. But what his employer didn't know was that he was using their car to do it with! I do remember on one occassion being a back seat passenger with my brothers Howard and Stephen as Maurice thrashed his company car around a 'driving test' course which were popular at the time. Against the stop watch, competitors reversed into spaces, did hand brake turns and drove as fast as they could along a slalom course, all laid out with straw bales on grass.

Sir Stirling and Maurice at Le Mans, 2009

His competition 'career' came to an abrupt end when he left the road during a rally and put the company car through a closed farm gate! That must have entailed a difficult conversation with the area manager, explaining how the Morris Oxford got damaged.

After that he confined his motorsport involvement to marshalling at events and taking me along with him to watch race meetings. The first of these was at Crystal Palace in 1953. I was a young child and went with my Dad, Maurice and my Grandad, Charlie. All was well with me during the warming up lap of the first race. However, when the actual race started it all changed and apparently I screamed the place down because of the noise. Worse still, I started kicking the man in front of us as I sat on Maurice's shoulders. We left early.

I did, however, get used to the noise over the next year or so and by 1955 we were going to race meetings regularly at Crystal Palace, Brands Hatch, Aintree and lesser known tracks like Brough Airfield and Oliver's Mount in Scarborough.
I was addicted.

Motor racing became an obsession. I couldn't get enough of it. But in those days the only time that the sport seemed to get a mention in the media was when a driver had been badly injured or worse. There were, of course, specialist magazines like Motor Sport and Motor Racing of which I was an avid reader whenever there was a copy of either in the house. There was minimal TV coverage in those days, but that didn't matter as we didn't always have a TV! So the best way to feed my addiction was by being taken by my Dad, Maurice, often accompanied by my Grandad, Charlie, to meetings and see the racing first hand.

Then I was given an autograph book for my birthday and with the drivers being so accessible in those days I felt I could get involved with the sport in a small way.

Scruffy as it now is, my autograph book is one of my most prized possessions and has been for more than 60 years! So when Andrew Marriott suggested using it as the basis for a book I thought it was a great idea. I have subsequently spent hours looking through old race programmes which I have also kept all this time and which I have used as a source of background information. I have also found some family photos taken at the time. All bar one of the black and white ones were taken by Charlie.

I have not attempted to clean up any of the archive material used in this book. I think that it would be wrong to do so. It is what it is. As a result the images from my autograph book, programmes and family photos in this book are in 'a warts and all' condition. That includes smudges, torn pages, finger prints and my awful hand writing. My personal stories in this book are events that happened a long time ago. But because of how much my book has meant to me for all these years, the stories that the signatures evoke are still fresh in mind. This book has also presented me with the extremely pleasant task of illustrating some of the events that I have witnessed first hand and others that I wish I had been able to witness.

I don't want the following to sound like one of those crass narcisstic speeches one hears so-called celebs making at award ceremonies. So here goes; I would like to thank Charlie and Maurice for showing me the light all those years ago. To Andrew Marriott for suggesting doing the book. I am also ever grateful to my partner Stella for her patience during the production of this book and the fact that she has again had to put on hold the paintings of flowers that I said I would paint for her one day.

Finally I would like to say a retrospective thank you to all those 'real racers' who obligingly signed my autograph book more than half a century ago.

Martin Tomlinson
Duxford 2022

Third generation enthusiast: Me with a Maserati, Crystal Palace, 1959

... and fouth generation: Sam with a Maserati, Goodwood, 1995

BRANDS HATCH

I'm not sure how many times I have been to Brands Hatch. It's such a wonderful circuit and evokes many memories every time I visit it.

One of my earliest memories of Brands was in 1956 and seeing a certain G. Hill driving a yellow Lotus XI. This was very early in his career and on a number of occasions we saw him leave the circuit on the bend which is now called Surtees. It must have been due to his inexperience. But it didn't take long before Graham had things worked out!

Another early memory was feeling the ground shake as a full grid of F3 cars were revving their 500cc motor cycle engines seconds before the start of a race. Those who have experienced this are unlikely to forget it.

And then there was the Boxing Day meeting. It was cold and wet in 1959, but John Bolster kept the crowd entertained with his colourful commentating. We saw Jim Clark get beaten by Lotus boss, Colin Chapman after a race-long dice in their Lotus Elites. We also witnessed Clark's single seater debut in a Formula Junior Gemini. One of the highlights of the meeting though was to see Graham Hill driving around the circuit in a motorised bath!

In 1958 Maurice, Charlie and I went to Brands Hatch to see the Kentish 100 International Formula 2 meeting. MT

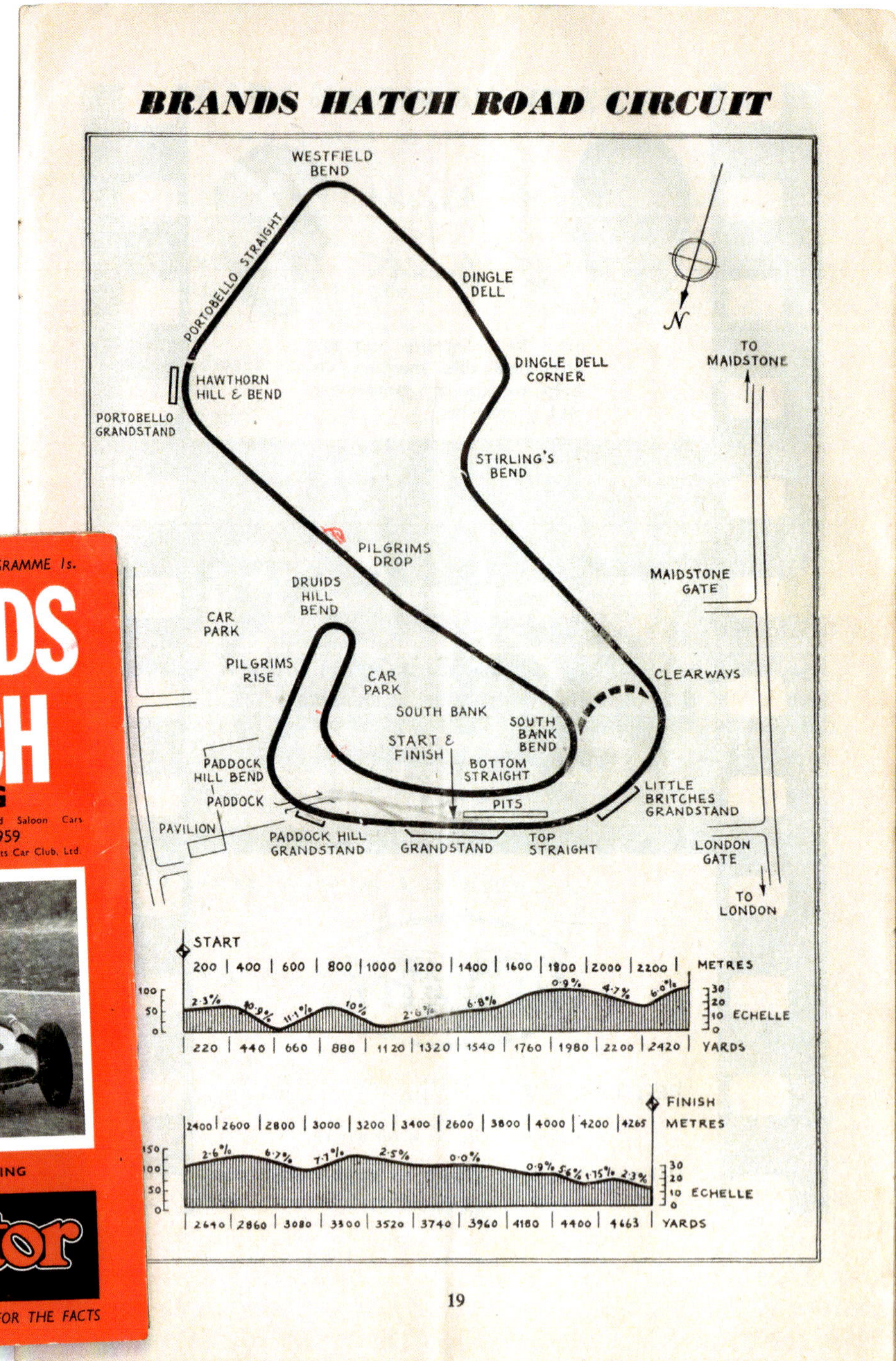

Event Six

Kentish "100" Trophy

For single seater racing cars complying with the International Formula Two. A qualifying event for the 1958 Autocar National Formula Two Championship

START 1.40 p.m. PART ONE 42 LAPS (52.08 miles)

No.	*Entrant*	*Driver*	*Car*	*c.c.*
1	Cooper Car Co. Ltd. *Surbiton, England*	J. Brabham .. *Sydney, Australia*	Cooper	1475
2	Cooper Car Co. Ltd *Surbiton, England*	R. Salvadori .. *Tolworth, England*	Cooper	1475
3	British Racing Partnership *London, W.C.2, England*	S. Lewis-Evans .. *Bexleyheath, England*	Cooper	1475
4	C. Libovitz .. *Bramley, England*	H. Schell .. *Cap d'Antibes, France*	Cooper	1475
5	Alan Brown .. *Guildford, England*	C. Shelby .. *Dallas, U.S.A.*	Cooper	1475
6	G. Wicken .. *Maidstone, England*	G. Wicken ..	Cooper	1475
7	R. R. C. Walker Racing Team *Dorking, England*	S. Moss .. *London, W.14, England*	Cooper	1475
8	R. R. C. Walker Racing Team *Dorking, England*	M. Trintignant .. *Gard, France*	Cooper	1475
9	J. Russell .. *Downham Market, England*	J. Russell ..	Cooper	1475
10	C. T. Atkins .. *Guildford, England*	I. Burgess .. *Guildford, England*	Cooper	1475
11	B. McLaren .. *Auckland, New Zealand*	B. McLaren ..	Cooper	1475
12	Nixons' Garage Ltd. *Newcastle, England*	H. Taylor .. *Biggleswade, England*	Cooper	1475
14	Team Lotus .. *London, N.8, England*	G. Hill .. *London, N.W.3, England*	Lotus	1475
15	Team Lotus .. *London, N.8, England*	C. Allison .. *Brough, England*	Lotus	1475
16	Ecurie Demi-litre .. *Cheltenham, England*	I. Bueb .. *Cheltenham, England*	Lotus	1475
17	D. Taylor .. *London, S.E.9, England*	D. Taylor ..	Lotus	1475
	Reserves—			
18	S. H. Jensen .. *Palmerston North, New Zealand*	S. H. Jensen ..	Cooper	1475
19	J. Fisher .. *Portsmouth, England*	~~L. Leston~~ .. *London, N.W.8, England*	Lotus	1475

USE LAP CHART OVERLEAF

23

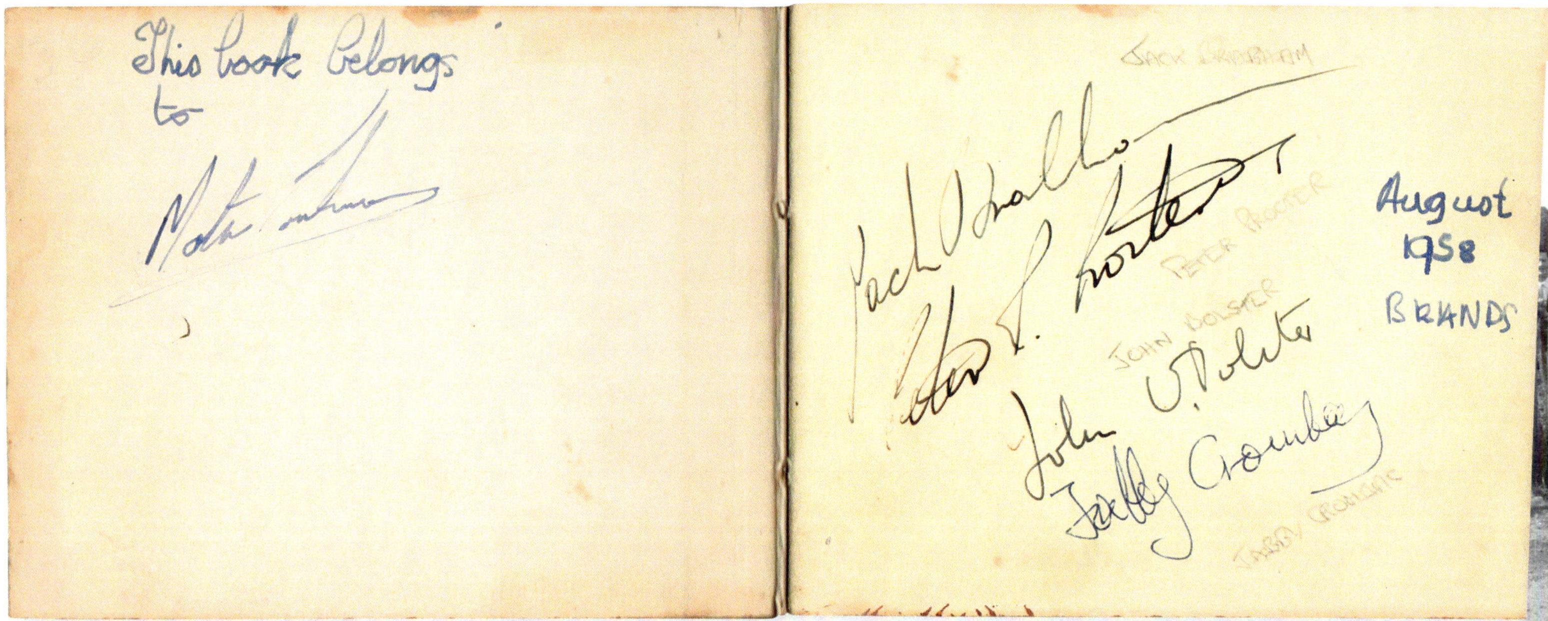

John Bolster, Brands Hatch, 1958

Jack Brabham

Jack Brabham was a three-times World Champion and the first man to win a World Championship race driving a car of his own name. John Arthur Brabham, always known as Jack, was a former Royal Australian Air Force flight mechanic and raced oval midget cars out of his small engineering workshop in Sydney. Later he bought a Cooper-Bristol which he raced successfully both at home and in NZ. So he headed for the UK where he bought another Cooper and quickly established a friendship with Charles and John Cooper.

He worked closely with the Cooper Car Company where his talents both as an engineer and driver were quickly recognised. Aged 29 he made his Grand Prix debut at Silverstone while also successfully racing the Cooper "Bobtail" sportscars.

In 1956 he became an official Cooper driver racing in both F1 and F2 in an age when rear-engined cars were starting to edge out those with the engine at the front. His first Grand Prix victory came in 1959 in the season opening Monaco GP – his Cooper now equipped with a 2.5 litre engine, previously only smaller units were available. He sped to the World Championship that year and followed it up by taking a second title the following year.

He then set up his own racing car construction company with Ron Tauranac and raced Formula 1 for another nine seasons. The first time win for a Brabham driven by Brabham at the French GP at Reims in 1966 set him up for his third World title that year and he was was runner-up the following season. He was knighted in 1978 and his three sons all followed in his racing footsteps. ARM

Peter Procter

Yorkshireman Peter Proctor was a former British Champion cyclist who became a great motor sport all-rounder equally at home in the Monte Carlo Rally, the Le Mans 24 Hours or single-seaters. He logged up victories in Formula Junior and had a couple of F2 podiums. At 92, he is a regular spectator at Silverstone and still carries the scars of a fiery accident at Goodwood in a Ford Anglia. ARM

John Bolster

Bolster was an eccentric former racer who became probably the first ever TV pits reporter although his fruity language finally got the deer-stalker hatted Bolster the sack from the BBC. He was also a leading journalist and road tester and was, for many years, the Technical Editor of Autosport magazine. ARM

Jabby Crombac

Anglophile Gerard "Jabby" Crombac founded the magazine Sport Auto and was considered the finest French racing journalist of his time. He was friendly with Jim Clark and Colin Chapman and wrote definitive biography on the latter. ARM

Jack Brabham wins the 1966 French GP at Reims. In doing so became the first driver to win a F1 GP in a car of his own construction. Brabham then went on to win the British, Dutch and German GP's and subsequently the 1966 drivers and constructors World Championships. MT.

SHELL
SHELL
12

The Tale of the Melting Ice Lolly

On 30th August 1958 I was let loose in the Brands Hatch paddock armed with my new autograph book, fountain pen and a pencil. I was just eight years old and had come with Maurice but he was off marshalling. So I was left to wander the paddock on my own, it didn't seem to matter in those days, in my schoolboy quest to track down my heroes and start filling my pristine autograph book.

Jack Brabham was the first, a pretty good start by any standard. Soon afterwards I came across Graham Hill who was eating an orange ice lolly. The obliging Hill asked me to hold his ice lolly while he signed my book. It was a hot day and the ice lolly started to melt all over my hand. I hadn't really noticed, being otherwise engaged in gawping up at this famous racing driver as he signed my book. Hill though had noticed the sticky mess that his melted ice lolly had made on my hand and suggested that I should get cleaned up. So he took me to the drivers' changing room which in those days was a wooden shack at the top of the paddock where the Kentagon now stands. Once inside he took me over to a sink and found me some soap and a towel.

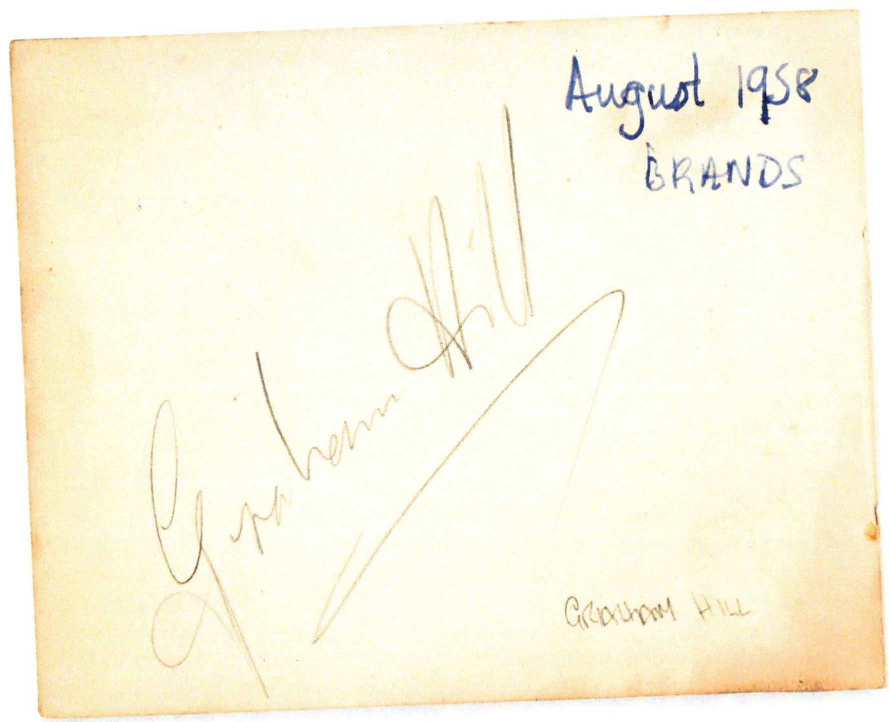

Whilst I was drying myself none other than Stirling Moss and Harry Schell walked in. At which point Hill picked up my dripping flannel and threw it across the room, hitting Schell on the side of his face. He then called out to the two other drivers, something along the lines of "sign the boy's book". This they did and the outcome of this can be seen on page 10 overleaf. Can you imagine that happening nowadays!

Small wonder Graham Hill was always a great favourite of mine. But what a start to my autograph collection - four Grand Prix drivers in the first couple of hours! MT

Graham Hill

With his twinkly eyes and bristling moustache Graham Hill looked every bit a matinee idol. Although he didn't learn to drive until he was 24, the Hampstead - born Hill quickly took to racing when he saw an advertisement for some laps of Brands Hatch in a Cooper Formula 3 car in 1954.

The former Naval Petty Officer joined Team Lotus as a mechanic but it didn't take him long to talk his way into the cockpit and he made his debut for the team at the 1958 Monaco GP. This was the start of an extraordinary career which saw him win at the Monegasque track no fewer than five times. He moved from Lotus to BRM where he won his first World Championship in 1962, later moving back to Lotus where he took his second title in 1968. Subsequently he raced for Brabham and then set up his own Embassy Hill team and retired in 1975.

Not only did he win 14 GPs, he became the only man to win motorsports' Triple Crown - The Monaco Grand Prix/World Championship, the Indianapolis 500 (1966) and the Le Mans 24 Hours (1972) for Matra.

Prior to racing he had been a competitive rower. He wore the colours of the London Rowing Club on his crash helmet and met his wife Betty whilst rowing. His infectious and cheeky personality made him a popular TV guest and he was a BBC Sports Personality of the Year.

His son Damon went on to win the World Championship in 1995 thus becoming the only father and son to achieve this feat. By then Graham had died when the Piper Aztec, light aircraft he was flying crashed in fog near Elstree in November 1975. ARM

In his own opinion the 1965 Monaco GP was Graham Hill's greatest race. Early on in the race, whilst leading, Hill had gone down the escape road at the chicane to avoid a back-marker. He climbed out of his BRM and pushed it back onto the track to rejoin in fifth place and set off after the leaders who were over half a minute up the road! Undaunted, Hill gradually reduced the gap and eventually passed Lorenzo Bandini's Ferrari to re-take the lead on lap 65 which he kept until the chequered flag. MT

3
17

Stirling Moss

Signing autographs at Brands Hatch, 1960

For most motor racing autograph collectors, the signature they most wanted in their book was that of Stirling Moss. Martin was not alone. But Stirling, true professional that he was, was always hugely obliging and knew the power of the pubic. Indeed he became sysonymous as Mr Motor Racing, although he never won the World Championship – coming close several times and had more recent point tariffs been in place he would have taken the title. The son of dentist Alfred Moss, Stirling was a teenage prodigy and was soon dominating the 500 cc Formula 3 category as well as winning the RAC Tourist Trophy in a Jaguar XX120.

He won some 16 World Championship races for teams such as Mercedes Benz, Maserati, Vanwall and latterly with Rob Walker's independent team. Indeed with the Walker Lotus 18 he scored what many considered his finest win at the 1961 Monaco Grand Prix. But other great wins included his success in the 1955 British Grand Prix when he just edged out Mercedes team mate Fangio to the chequered flag.

Moss was also a great all-rounder and had success in many different categories, high-lighted by his win in the 1955 Mille Miglia also for Mercedes. He was a highly accomplished rally driver and also broke land speed records.

Moss' professional career-ending Goodwood crash was front page news and after his recovery he became what is sometime known as a "national treasure". He did return to racing mainly in his historic events and fans still queued for his autograph. He died aged 90 in 2020. ARM

Harry Schell

Although born in Paris, Harry Schell had American motor racing parents. His father raced but was killed in a road accident. His heiress mother went on to run cars at the Indianapolis 500. After racing sportscars he became the first American to start in the World Championship when he competed in the 1950 Monaco Grand Prix. His career spanned ten seasons and he raced firstly as a privateer but later in his career for Gordini, Ferrari, Vanwall, Maserati and BRM. Racing for BRM was the closest he got to a World Championship win when he finished second in the 1958 Dutch GP. He was killed aged 38, practising for the 1960 Silverstone International Trophy. ARM

Harry Schell, Vanwall, Crystal Palace, 30th July 1955

"1961 Monaco GP" was Sir Stirling's emphatic response to my question of what he considered was his greatest race.

In a year old, privately entered, Lotus 18 with a 40bhp engine deficit on his main rivals, Moss won by 3.7 seconds from Richie Ginther's Ferrari. Such was the pace of the race that Moss' lap average for the 100 laps was only four tenths of a second slower than his pole position qualifying time of 1m39.1! MT

20
36

The Who's Who of 1950's Formula 3

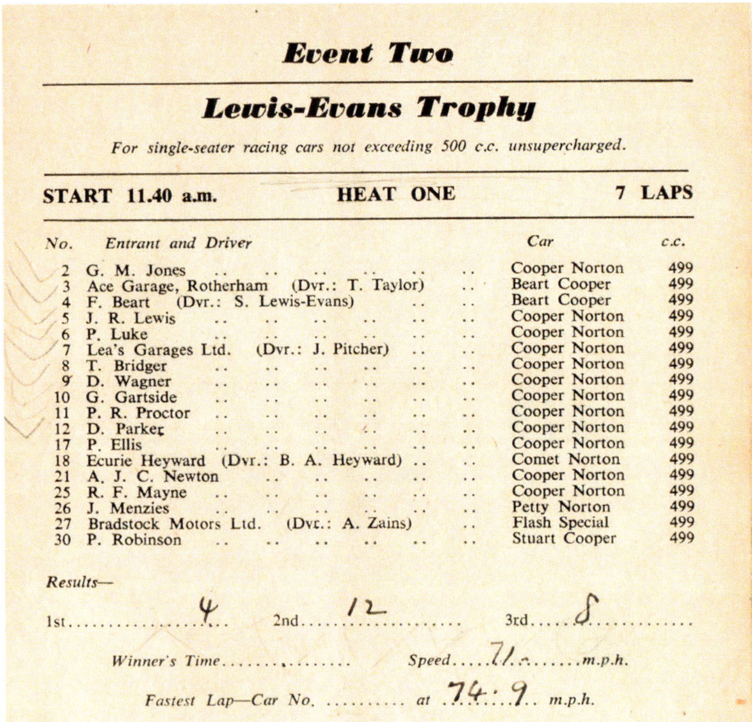

Event Two

Lewis-Evans Trophy

For single-seater racing cars not exceeding 500 c.c. unsupercharged.

START 11.40 a.m. **HEAT ONE** **7 LAPS**

No.	Entrant and Driver	Car	c.c.
2	G. M. Jones	Cooper Norton	499
3	Ace Garage, Rotherham (Dvr.: T. Taylor)	Beart Cooper	499
4	F. Beart (Dvr.: S. Lewis-Evans)	Beart Cooper	499
5	J. R. Lewis	Cooper Norton	499
6	P. Luke	Cooper Norton	499
7	Lea's Garages Ltd. (Dvr.: J. Pitcher)	Cooper Norton	499
8	T. Bridger	Cooper Norton	499
9	D. Wagner	Cooper Norton	499
10	G. Gartside	Cooper Norton	499
11	P. R. Proctor	Cooper Norton	499
12	D. Parker	Cooper Norton	499
17	P. Ellis	Cooper Norton	499
18	Ecurie Heyward (Dvr.: B. A. Heyward)	Comet Norton	499
21	A. J. C. Newton	Cooper Norton	499
25	R. F. Mayne	Cooper Norton	499
26	J. Menzies	Petty Norton	499
27	Bradstock Motors Ltd. (Dvr.: A. Zains)	Flash Special	499
30	P. Robinson	Stuart Cooper	499

Results—

1st ....4........ 2nd ....12........ 3rd ....8........

Winner's Time .... *Speed* ....71.... *m.p.h.*

Fastest Lap—Car No. .... *at* ....74:9.... *m.p.h.*

500cc Formula 3 Racing

As Britain emerged from the devastation of WW2, racers looked round for a cheap single-seater category as a first-stepping stone on the way to Formula 1. The answer was lightweight cars powered by a 500 cc motorcycle engine which were readily available. Officially recognised as Formula 3 there were soon many willing constructors and drivers.

The engines of choice were mainly Norton or the Speedway JAP engine, usually mounted behind the driver – something that had not been see since the pre-war Auto Union Grand Prix cars. However there were also front-engined cars. Charles Cooper's cars were soon to dominate the category although the Kiefts, JBS and Emerysons were all quick on their day.

Many top drivers learned the ropes in these cars in the 1950s with Stirling Moss the best known and most successful. But other drivers like Stuart Lewis-Evans, Ivor Bueb, Jim Russell, Peter Collins and even Ken Tyrrell and Bernie Ecclestone raced the cars. But if Stirling wasn't winning it was usually a man called Don Parker. ARM

Stuart Lewis-Evans

A second generation racer, Stuart Lewis-Evans was an emerging talent whose life was cruelly cut short, aged 28, when he crashed in the Moroccan GP in a Vanwall. He was air-lifted back to the UK but died six days later from the burns. Lewis-Evans had emerged from 500 cc F3 racing and after a strong fourth place at Monaco in his debut Grand Prix for Connaught was snapped up by the Vanwall team. Tony Vandervell considered him to have equal skill to that of Moss. In his second season with the team in 1958 the Bernie Ecclestone-managed driver finished third in Belgium and Portugal. But then in the final race of the year tragedy struck. ARM

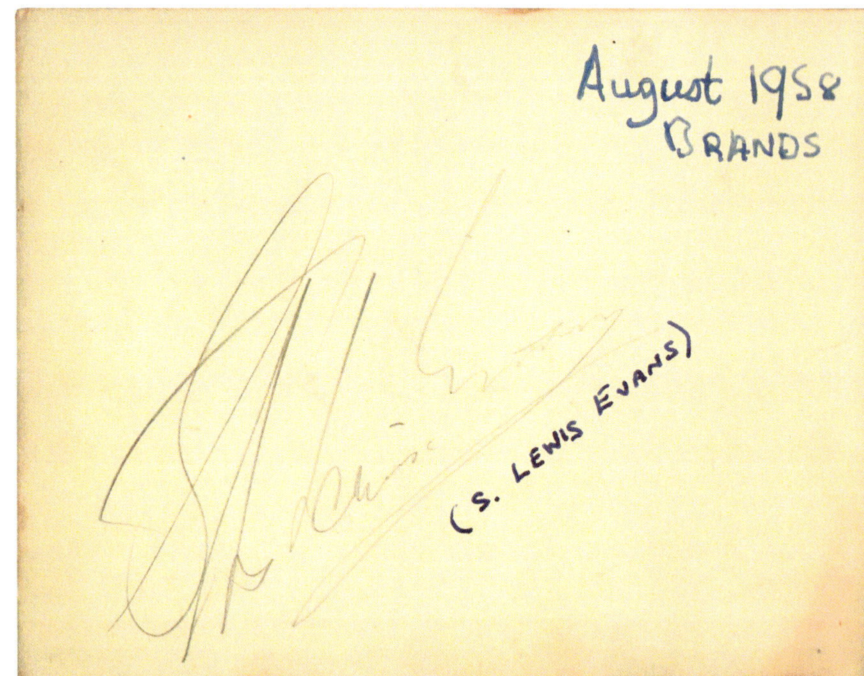

Don Parker won more F3 races than any other driver in the 1950's. This is his self-built Parker 500

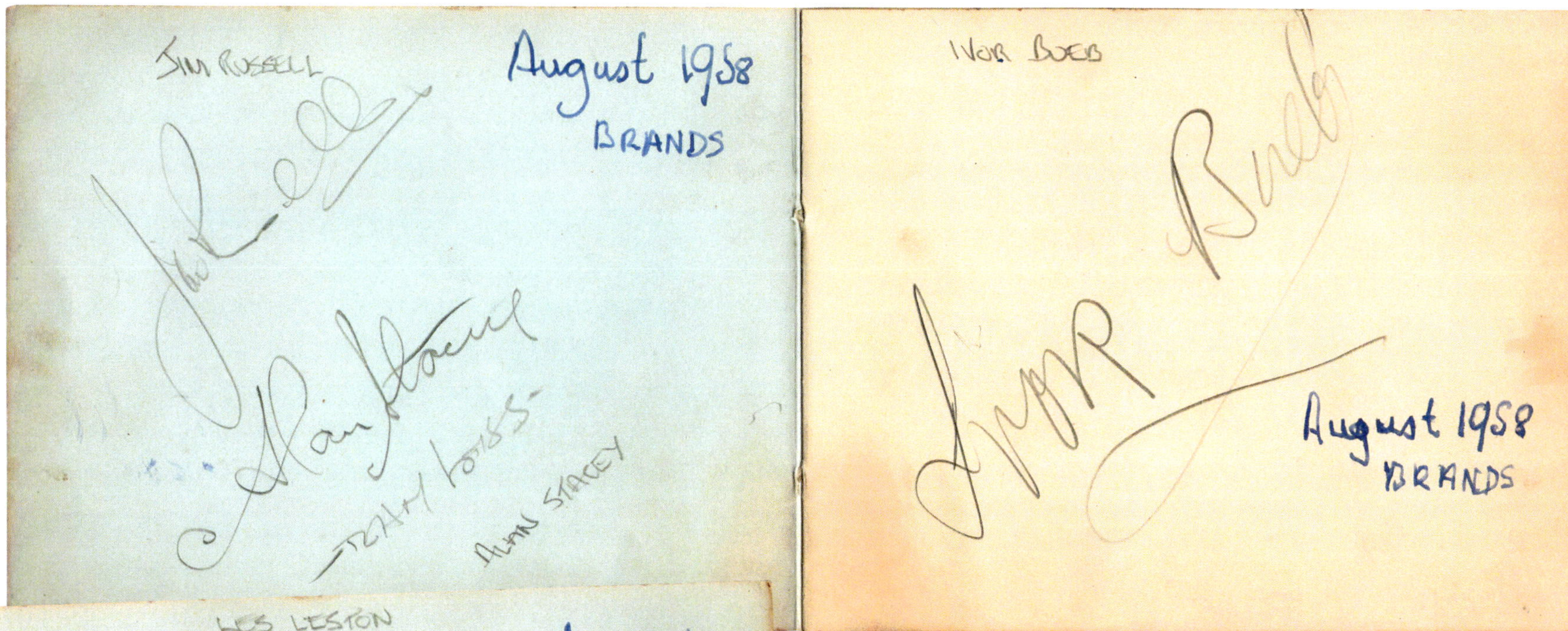

Jim Russell

Jim Russell was born above his parents' fish and chip shop near the Snetterton track. He grew up to run a successful garage business but didn't begin racing until he was 32 in the emerging 500cc Formula 3 category. He won the British F3 Championship in 1955,6 & 7 as well as sportscars races. He won at Formula 2 level but then his career was cut short after a serious accident at Le Mans in 1959. But he is best known as the pioneer of motor racing schools, starting at Snetterton but the operation grew to embrace several countries. Its graduates included Emerson Fittipaldi, Derek Bell, and Jacques Villeneuve amongst many others. In 1966 he was heavily involved in John Frankenheimer's famous film Grand Prix, both training actors like James Garner to race, but also providing many of the cars. Later in life he ran a stud farm and died in 2019, just two years short of 100. ARM

Les Leston

Leston was best known as the man who commercialised the selling of race suits and other equipment such as pit-boards but he was also a jazz musician and fine driver. He briefly drove in Formula 1 for Connaught, Cooper and BRM. But he was best known for racing his Lotus Elite with the reg' number DAD10. ARM.

Ivor Bueb

Ivor Bueb was a two-times winner of the Le Mans 24 Hours in Jaguar D-types. His first victory came for the Jaguar team when he partnered Mike Hawthorn to victory in the tragic 1955 race. The following year, again with Hawthorn, he was third and then in 1957 he shared the Ecurie Ecosse success with Ron Flockhart. The Essex-born driver also raced briefly in Formula 1 for the Connaught team and privateers in the late-50s. ARM

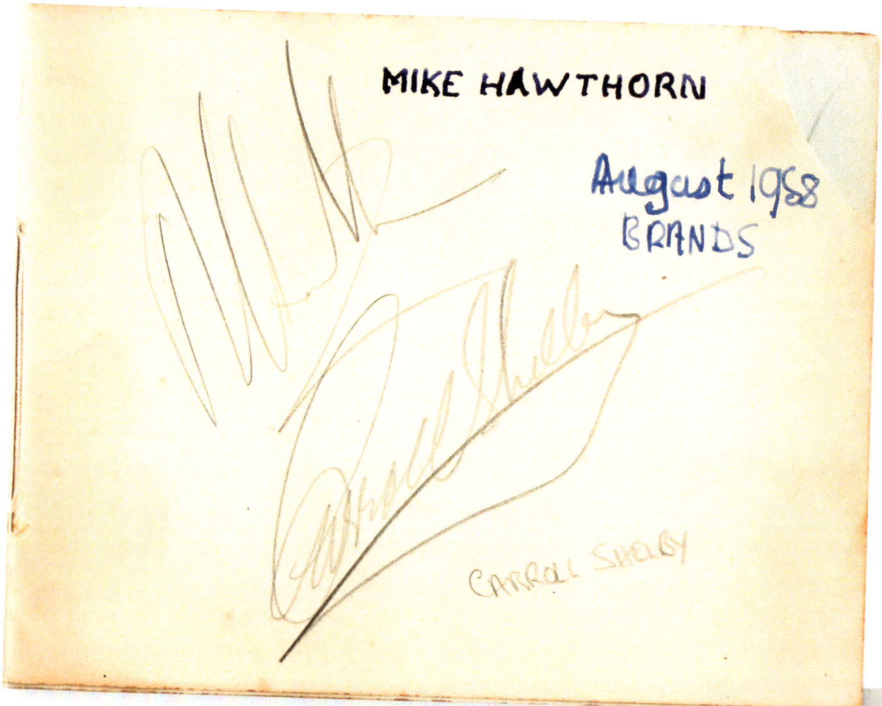

Mike Hawthorn

Mike Hawthorn wrote his name in the history books as Britain's first World Champion after a battle for the 1958 title with rival Stirling Moss. He started in sportscars and the Yorkshire-born but Surrey-based Hawthorn first made his mark at the Brighton Speed Trials - an event that still exists to this day. There followed a string of victories, mainly at Goodwood in a Cooper-Bristol.

The switch to single-seaters in 1952 brought Hawthorn – who often raced wearing a spotted bow-tie – to the attention of Enzo Ferrari, who signed him for the 1953 World Championship season. He quickly repaid the Commendatore's faith in him with a victory over Fangio in the 1953 French GP at Reims – in a race where the first four drivers finished virtually nose to tail. He finished fourth in the World Championship that year, a great result for a "rookie". The following year he went one better finishing third after winning the last race of the season in Spain.

Like many of the drivers of that era he also raced in other categories and he drove for both Ferrari and Jaguar at Le Mans. He won with Ivor Bueb for the Coventry firm in 1955 in the tragic race where over 80 spectators were killed and in which he was implemented as a possible cause.

His final season with Ferrari in 1958 saw just a single victory in France but second place at the telegraph-post lined Morocco track edged him to the title. Hawthorn promptly announced his retirement from the sport acutely aware of the dangers having lost several close friends including Peter Collins. Ironically he was then to lose his own life in a Jaguar saloon just three months later. ARM

Mike Hawthorn, Ferrari 'Squalo', Spanish GP, 1954

Carroll Shelby, Brands Hatch, 30 August 1958 (Autographed in 1996) Could that be Ian 'Puddle Jumper' Raby standing next to the bus?

In 1950's Britain you were either a Stirling Moss fan or a Mike Hawthorn fan. I was one of the latter.

In 1958 Mike Hawthorn became the first Britain to win the World Championship. Here he is about to leave the pits during practice for the season's final race, the Moroccan GP in which he finished second. In doing so he clinched the crown by a single point from Moss. MT

6

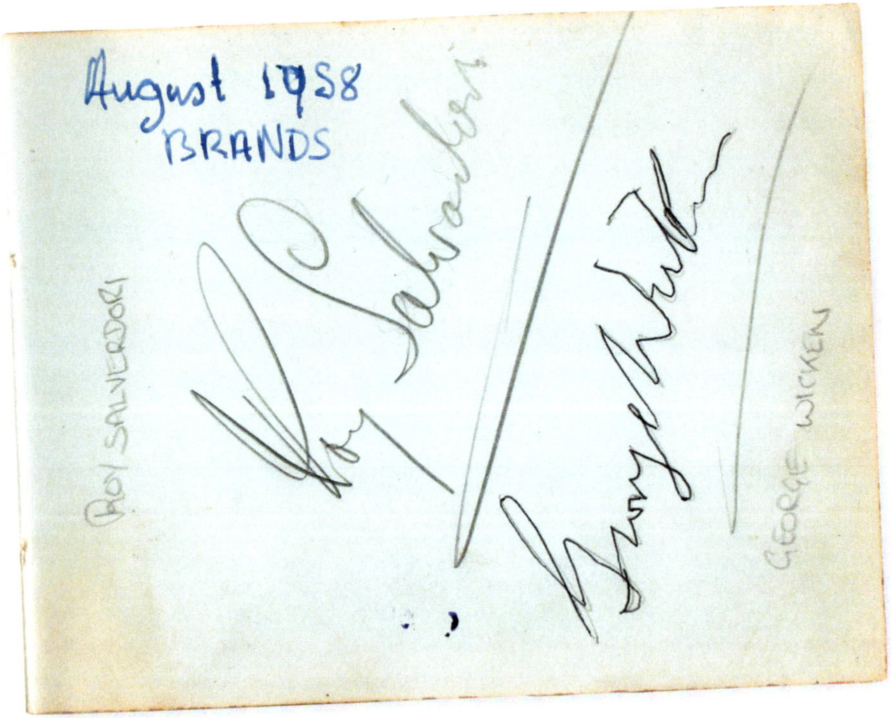

King of The Palace

During a picture signing at Goodwood (photo on page 70), I mentioned to Roy Salvadori that I had seen him win four races in one day at Crystal Palace which I thought was quite something. He had indeed done so on 22 May 1961 - The London Trophy F1 race (Cooper Climax), The Norbury Trophy (E Type Jaguar), The Green Helmet Trophy (Cooper Monaco) and the saloon car race in John Coombs' 3.8 Jaguar MkII.

Salvadori responded "Well it wasn't that difficult. really. I just made sure that all the fast boys were racing somewhere else on that day before I put my entries in for the Palace." MT

Roy Salvadori

Roy was a British racer with an Italian heritage and was a great all-rounder at home as much in a Formula 1 car as a sportscar. He made his Formula 1 debut in 1952 and competed at the top level for ten years driving for Cooper, Vanwall, BRM, Aston Martin and Connaught. While he won a number of non-championship Formula 1 races his best World Championship finish was second in the 1958 German GP for Cooper.

He competed in eleven Le Mans 24 Hours, usually for Aston Martin and won the 1959 race with Carroll Shelby in 1959 in the DBR1, was third the following year sharing with Jim Clark and won his class in 1963 in a Cunningham Jaguar E-type. He also has a lot of success racing Jaguar saloons. After hanging up his helmet he turned to team management. He died aged 90. ARM

Maurice Trintignant

Trintignant was one of France's finest racers who won both the 1958 Monaco GP for Rob Walker and Le Mans for Ferrari in 1954. He was also a wine-maker and worried not about his nickname Le Petoulet - rat droppings which blocked the fuel system of one of his cars. ARM

Maurice Trintignant, Cooper Climax, Monaco GP, 1958

George Wicken

George was a teetotal, religious man who ran the family dairy business in Kent. After success in 500 cc Formula 3 racing, he competed in Formula 2 with a Cooper-Climax from 1957 to 1960. ARM

The London Trophy F1 race at London's Crystal Palace circuit on 22 May 1961. Roy Salvadori (Cooper) leads Henry Taylor (Lotus). MT

Brands Hatch Circuit Ltd didn't mind lashing out on the event advertising!

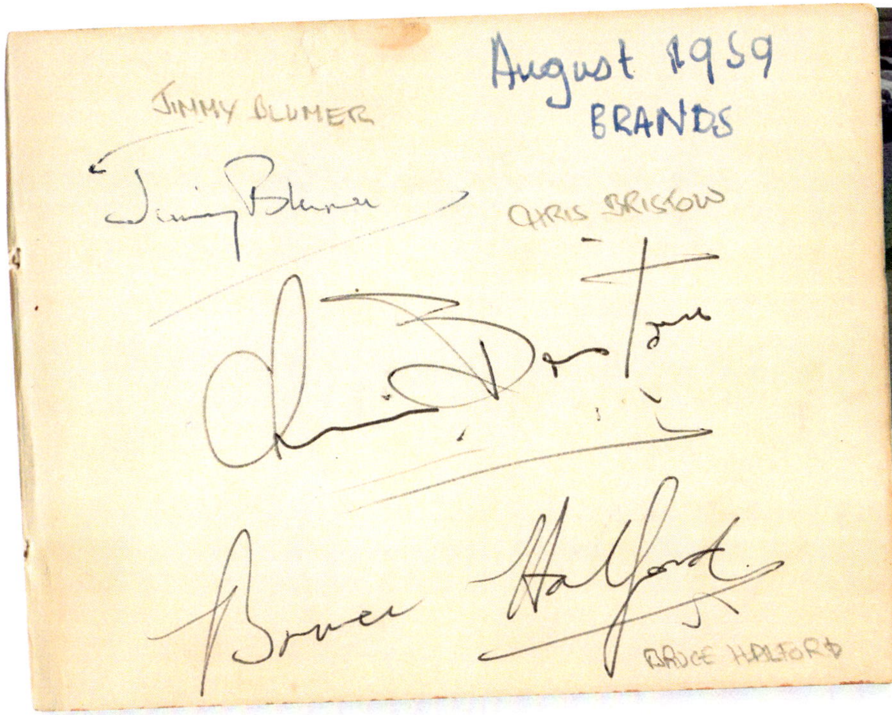

Chris Bristow's British Racing Partnership F2 Cooper Borgward, Brands Hatch, 1959.

Alan Stacey working on his F2 Lotus 16 Climax, Brands Hatch, 1959

Chris Bristow, British Racing Partnership F1 Cooper, Goodwood, Easter Monday 1960

Jimmy Blumer

Darlington's Jimmy Blumer was an extrovert racer who was a private pilot and well known aerial photographer. He made headlines when he took part in the Monte Carlo Rally, aged 18, but he made his mark winning regularly in Cooper Monaco sportscars in the 1960s. He was also a leading saloon car racer and won the Brands Hatch 6hrs with Mike Parkes in a Jaguar Mk2. ARM

1960 Belgian GP

Held at Spa-Francorchamps on June 19th, 1960 this was a desperately tragic race for British drivers. In practice both Stirling Moss and Mike Taylor were seriously injured, but worse was to come in the race itself. Two rising British talents Chris Bristow and Alan Stacey perished in separate incidents. Bristow crashed and was thrown out of his Cooper into a barbed wire fence, Stacey was hit in the face by a bird and the subsequent fiery crash killed him. Both had autographed Martin's book. ARM

Bruce Halford

Bruce Halford was a privateer Formula 1 racer who competed mainly in his own Maserati 250F in the late 1950s. He had limited success in some minor non-championship races and later raced a Cooper, Emeryson and a Lotus 16. With the latter he tasted success fifty years later in historic events. In period he was successful in a Lister-Jaguar sportscar and he survived being thrown out of a Cooper Monaco at Le Mans. ARM.

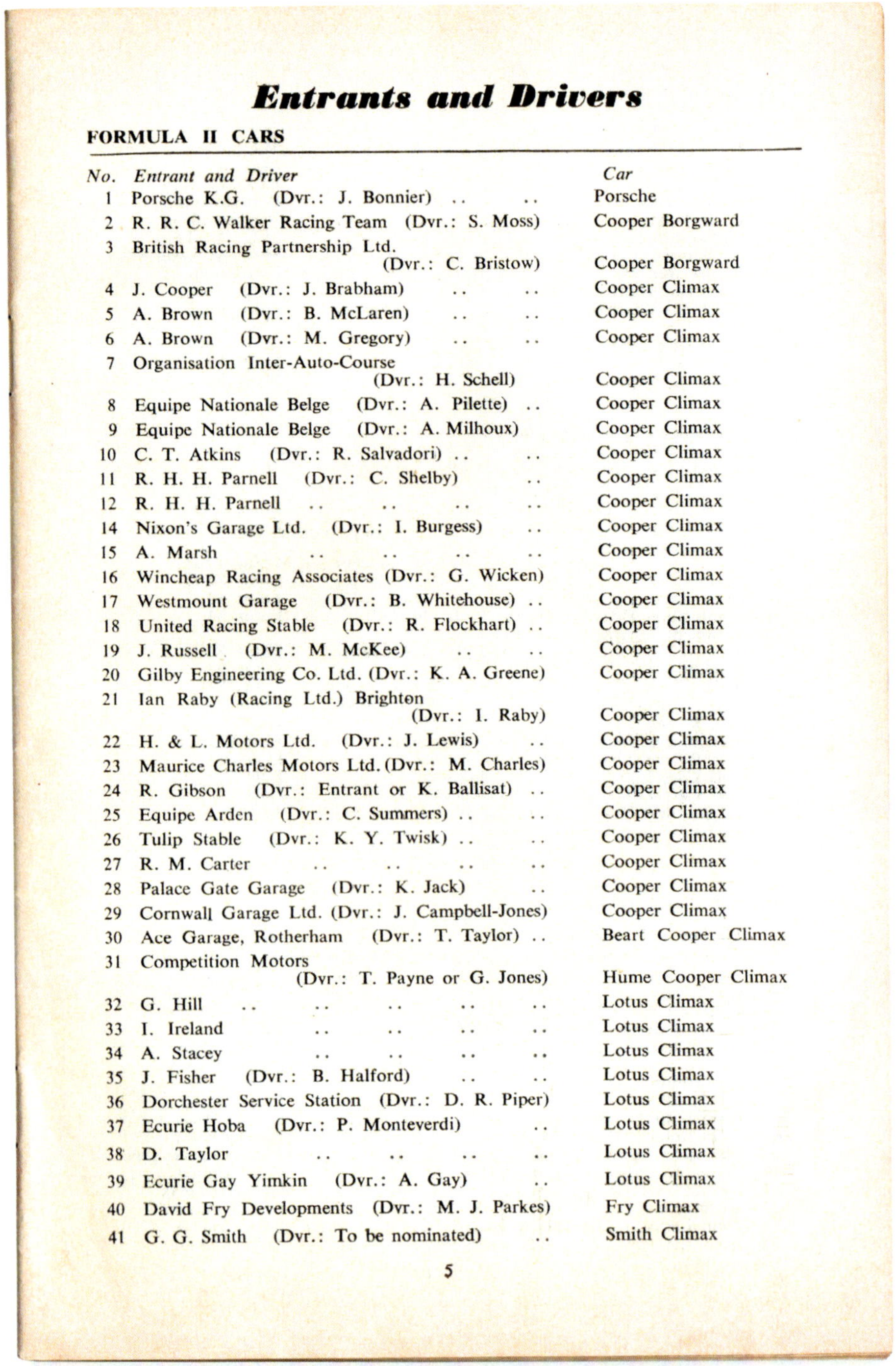

Entrants and Drivers

FORMULA II CARS

No.	Entrant and Driver	Car
1	Porsche K.G. (Dvr.: J. Bonnier)	Porsche
2	R. R. C. Walker Racing Team (Dvr.: S. Moss)	Cooper Borgward
3	British Racing Partnership Ltd. (Dvr.: C. Bristow)	Cooper Borgward
4	J. Cooper (Dvr.: J. Brabham)	Cooper Climax
5	A. Brown (Dvr.: B. McLaren)	Cooper Climax
6	A. Brown (Dvr.: M. Gregory)	Cooper Climax
7	Organisation Inter-Auto-Course (Dvr.: H. Schell)	Cooper Climax
8	Equipe Nationale Belge (Dvr.: A. Pilette) ..	Cooper Climax
9	Equipe Nationale Belge (Dvr.: A. Milhoux)	Cooper Climax
10	C. T. Atkins (Dvr.: R. Salvadori)	Cooper Climax
11	R. H. H. Parnell (Dvr.: C. Shelby) ..	Cooper Climax
12	R. H. H. Parnell	Cooper Climax
14	Nixon's Garage Ltd. (Dvr.: I. Burgess) ..	Cooper Climax
15	A. Marsh	Cooper Climax
16	Wincheap Racing Associates (Dvr.: G. Wicken)	Cooper Climax
17	Westmount Garage (Dvr.: B. Whitehouse) ..	Cooper Climax
18	United Racing Stable (Dvr.: R. Flockhart) ..	Cooper Climax
19	J. Russell (Dvr.: M. McKee)	Cooper Climax
20	Gilby Engineering Co. Ltd. (Dvr.: K. A. Greene)	Cooper Climax
21	Ian Raby (Racing Ltd.) Brighton (Dvr.: I. Raby)	Cooper Climax
22	H. & L. Motors Ltd. (Dvr.: J. Lewis) ..	Cooper Climax
23	Maurice Charles Motors Ltd. (Dvr.: M. Charles)	Cooper Climax
24	R. Gibson (Dvr.: Entrant or K. Ballisat) ..	Cooper Climax
25	Equipe Arden (Dvr.: C. Summers)	Cooper Climax
26	Tulip Stable (Dvr.: K. Y. Twisk)	Cooper Climax
27	R. M. Carter	Cooper Climax
28	Palace Gate Garage (Dvr.: K. Jack) ..	Cooper Climax
29	Cornwall Garage Ltd. (Dvr.: J. Campbell-Jones)	Cooper Climax
30	Ace Garage, Rotherham (Dvr.: T. Taylor) ..	Beart Cooper Climax
31	Competition Motors (Dvr.: T. Payne or G. Jones)	Hume Cooper Climax
32	G. Hill	Lotus Climax
33	I. Ireland	Lotus Climax
34	A. Stacey	Lotus Climax
35	J. Fisher (Dvr.: B. Halford)	Lotus Climax
36	Dorchester Service Station (Dvr.: D. R. Piper)	Lotus Climax
37	Ecurie Hoba (Dvr.: P. Monteverdi) ..	Lotus Climax
38	D. Taylor	Lotus Climax
39	Ecurie Gay Yimkin (Dvr.: A. Gay) ..	Lotus Climax
40	David Fry Developments (Dvr.: M. J. Parkes)	Fry Climax
41	G. G. Smith (Dvr.: To be nominated) ..	Smith Climax

5

Take a close look at the team name for car number 7. It had to be Harry Schell's!

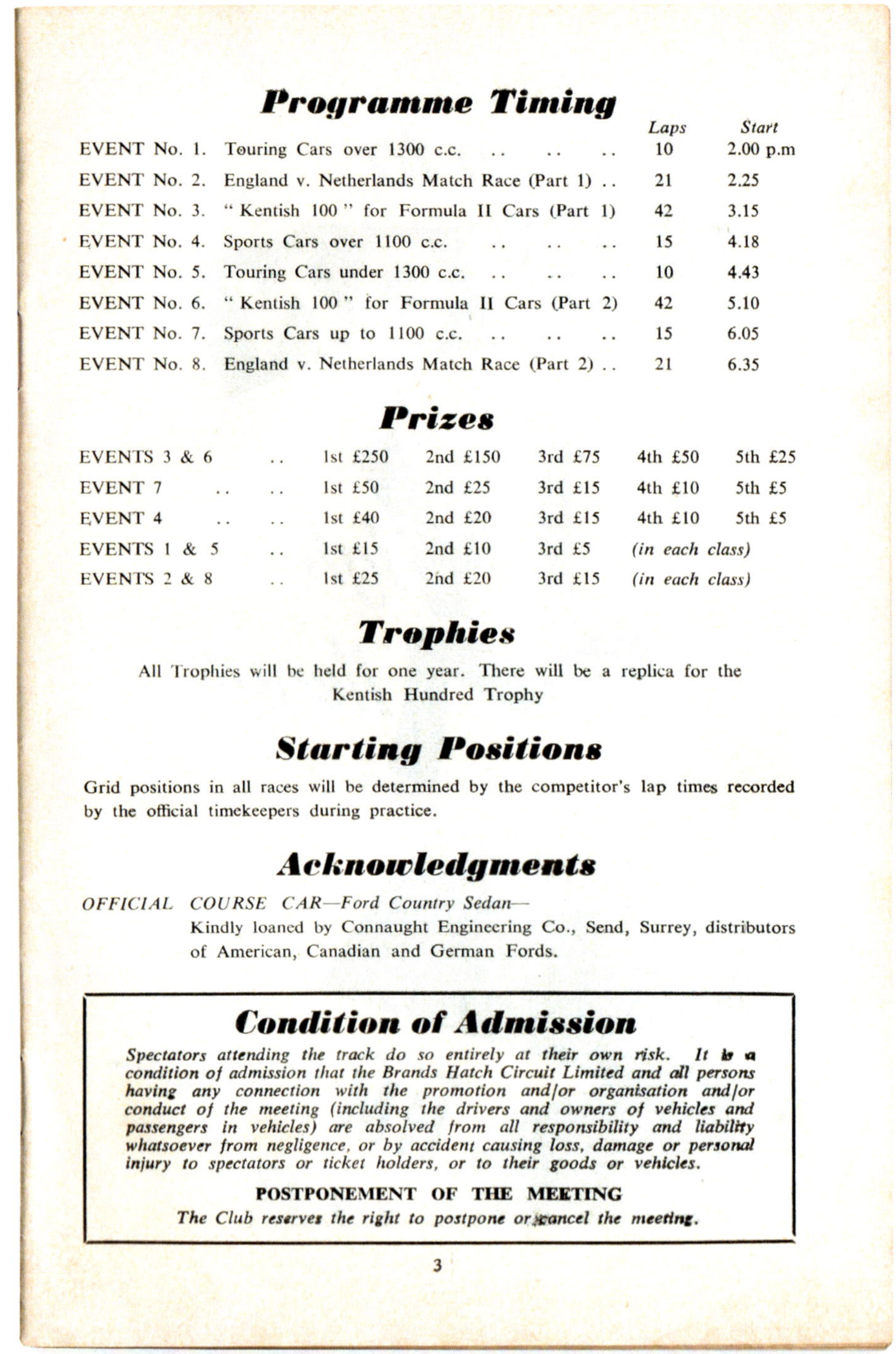

Programme Timing

		Laps	Start
EVENT No. 1.	Touring Cars over 1300 c.c.	10	2.00 p.m
EVENT No. 2.	England v. Netherlands Match Race (Part 1) ..	21	2.25
EVENT No. 3.	"Kentish 100" for Formula II Cars (Part 1)	42	3.15
EVENT No. 4.	Sports Cars over 1100 c.c.	15	4.18
EVENT No. 5.	Touring Cars under 1300 c.c.	10	4.43
EVENT No. 6.	"Kentish 100" for Formula II Cars (Part 2)	42	5.10
EVENT No. 7.	Sports Cars up to 1100 c.c.	15	6.05
EVENT No. 8.	England v. Netherlands Match Race (Part 2) ..	21	6.35

Prizes

EVENTS 3 & 6 ..	1st £250	2nd £150	3rd £75	4th £50	5th £25
EVENT 7	1st £50	2nd £25	3rd £15	4th £10	5th £5
EVENT 4	1st £40	2nd £20	3rd £15	4th £10	5th £5
EVENTS 1 & 5 ..	1st £15	2nd £10	3rd £5	*(in each class)*	
EVENTS 2 & 8 ..	1st £25	2nd £20	3rd £15	*(in each class)*	

Trophies

All Trophies will be held for one year. There will be a replica for the Kentish Hundred Trophy

Starting Positions

Grid positions in all races will be determined by the competitor's lap times recorded by the official timekeepers during practice.

Acknowledgments

OFFICIAL COURSE CAR—Ford Country Sedan—
Kindly loaned by Connaught Engineering Co., Send, Surrey, distributors of American, Canadian and German Fords.

Condition of Admission

Spectators attending the track do so entirely at their own risk. It is a condition of admission that the Brands Hatch Circuit Limited and all persons having any connection with the promotion and/or organisation and/or conduct of the meeting (including the drivers and owners of vehicles and passengers in vehicles) are absolved from all responsibility and liability whatsoever from negligence, or by accident causing loss, damage or personal injury to spectators or ticket holders, or to their goods or vehicles.

POSTPONEMENT OF THE MEETING

The Club reserves the right to postpone or cancel the meeting.

3

The prize money surely wouldn't have been the drivers only raison d'être for racing.

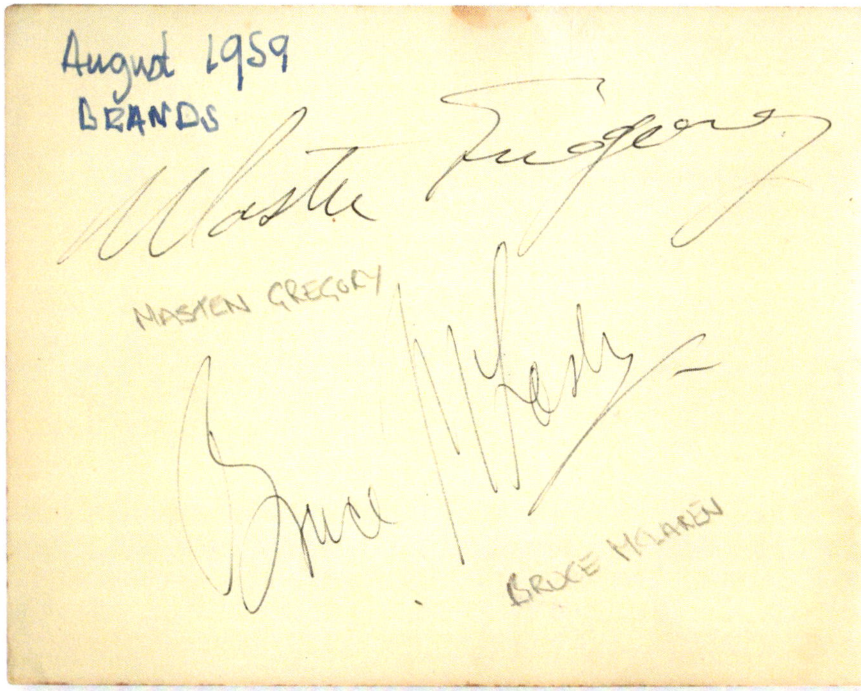

Masten Gregory

Masten Gregory was a bespectacled American who is probably best known for winning the 1965 Le Mans 24 Hours with Jochen Rindt in the NART Ferrari 250LM. But the man they called the Kansas City Flash, had an extensive Formula 1 career competing for some eight seasons. He made a spectacular debut taking the privateer Maserati 250F of Scuderia Cento Sud to third place at Monaco in 1957. But that was to be his finest result.

He mainly raced for privateer teams including UDT Laystall, Parnell Racing and again at the end of his career for Centro Sud. He also had a reputation for jumping out of cars when they were about to crash – particularly Listers. He died in Italy of a heart attack aged 53. ARM

Jo Bonnier's works F2 Porsche, Brands Hatch, 1959

Masten Gregory, NART Ferrari 250LM, winner (with Jochen Rindt) at Le Mans, 1965

Brief Encounters with Can Am Cars

In 1966 Snetterton circuit still included the Norwich Straight which ran parallel to the A11 trunk road. This, almost mile-long straight is where the 'Big Banger' sports cars like the McLarens and Lolas would probably have reached 170mph or more. It was only a couple of hundred, un-protected but for a hedgerow, yards from the trunk road.

On Good Friday 1966 we set off for Snetterton to see The Archie Scott Brown Memorial Trophy races for sports cars. Near to the circuit, we could hear the cars practising. And as we got to the trunk road just outside the circuit a bright orange McLaren, going in the same direction, shot passed us at full chat. The noise and proximity of the car was such a shock that for a split second we thought that Bruce had actually passed us on the road and not the nearby Norwich Straight.

On another occasion I was travelling with my mate Phil in his Mini Cooper S on our way to watch practice for the 1970 Race of Champions at Brands Hatch. As we got close to the circuit Phil looked in his mirror and shouted out "What the ...!" So I looked around to see what all the fuss was about. And there, just behind us was Bruce McLaren in his Can-Am M6A based, red M6GT road car!

Bruce had obviously spotted our reactions and gave us a mighty grin as he went past us like we were stood still. MT

Bruce McLaren

Born in Auckand, New Zealand Bruce McLaren was the man who gave his name to the McLaren Formula 1 team which continues to race to this day. His racing career quickly developed from driving an Austin 7 Special – which is exhibited at the McLaren factory – to a Formula 2 Coper. Rather like Jack Brabham he was both a fine engineer and talented driver.

Indeed it was Brabham who first spotted the young Kiwi as a future star. Aged just 21 Bruce won a Driver to Europe award with the opportunity to race a Formula 2 Cooper. Entered in the 1958 GP at the Nurburgring – F2 cars raced alongside the F1s – he finished an astounding fifth overall.

Cooper signed him to race alongside Brabham for 1959 and at the end of that year he won the US GP, at the time the youngest ever Grand Prix winner, a record which stood for four decades. A win in the 1962 Monaco GP cemented his reputation.

Drivers Briefing Brands Hatch, 30 August 1958
L - R: Bruce McLaren, Roy Salvadori and Innes Ireland

But just like Brabham, he then left Cooper to become a constructor in his own right, thus founding the company which went on to success in Formula 1 but also the Can-Am series which his cars dominated and Indianapolis where McLarens also won. Fellow Kiwi Denny Hulme joined him as team mate and also won for McLaren.

But his life was cut short at Goodwood in 1970 when the Can-Am car he was testing lost some bodywork and the car crashed into a marshal's post. But such was the organisation he had built, the McLaren team was able to continue racing successfully. ARM

Los Angeles GP, Riverside, 29 October 1967. Bruce McLaren in his M6A won the penultimate round and that year's CanAm Championship, after a battle with Jim Hall in the Chaparral. MT

4
66

This is how 10 year olds got into the paddock in 1960!

EVENT TWO

THE KENTISH HUNDRED TROPHY

For single-seater racing cars complying with the International Formula II

START 3.20 p.m. **40 LAPS**

No.	*Entrant and Driver*	*Car*	*c.c.*
2	Dr. Ing. h.c.F. Porsche KG. (Dvr.: G. Hill)	Porsche	1498
4	Dr. Ing. h.c.F. Porsche KG. (Dvr.: J. Bonnier)	Porsche	1498
6	R. R. C. Walker Racing Team (Dvr.: S. Moss)	Porsche	1498
8	C. T. Atkins (Dvr.: R. Salvadori)	Cooper-Climax	1475
10	Yeoman Credit Racing Team (Dvr.: ~~H. Taylor~~ or O. Gendebien)	Cooper-Climax	1475
12	N.Z.I.G.P. Racing Team (Dvr.: G. Lawton)	Cooper-Climax	1475
14	N.Z.I.G.P. Racing Team (Dvr.: D. Hulme)	Cooper-Climax	1475
16	J. Surtees	~~Cooper~~-Climax (LOTUS)	1475
18	John Fisher (Dvr.: B. Halford)	Cooper-Climax	1475
20	Alan Brown (Dvr.: ~~R. Flockhart~~)	Cooper-Climax	1475
22	J. Russell (Dvr.: M. McKee)	Cooper-Climax	1475
24	G. Wicken	Cooper-Climax	1475
26	R. H. Parnell	Cooper-Climax	1475
28	A. E. Marsh	Cooper-Climax	1475
30	J.B.W. Car Co, (Dvr.: S. Hart)	Cooper-Climax	1475
32	J. L. E. Ogier (Dvr.: J. Whitmore)	Cooper-Climax	1475
34	J. L. E. Ogier (Dvr.: A. Maggs *(Reserve)*	Cooper-Climax	1475
36	D.R.W. Engineering (Dvr.: ~~J. Campbell-Jones~~) *(Reserve)* D. PIPER.	Cooper-Climax	1475
38	G. Ashmore *(Reserve)*	Cooper-Climax	1475
40	H & L Motors Ltd. (Dvr.: J. R. Lewis) *(Reserve)*	Cooper-Climax	1475
42	Scuderia Centro-Sud (Dvr.: M. Gregory)	Cooper-Maserati	1484
44	Scuderia Centro-Sud (Dvr.: I. Burgess)	Lotus-Maserati	1484
46	Team Lotus (Dvr.: I. Ireland)	Lotus-Climax	1475
48	Team Lotus (Dvr.: J. Clark)	Lotus-Climax	1475
50	Mrs. L. Bryden-Brown (Dvr.: D. Gurney)	Lotus-Climax	1475
52	R. Parnell (Dvr.: G. Duke)	Lotus-Climax	1475
54	Team Thercel (Dvr.: N. R. Hicks)	Lotus-Climax	1475
56	Empire Cars (Brighton) Ltd. (Dvr.: I. E. Raby)	Hume Cooper-Climax	1475
58	Emeryson Cars Ltd. (Dvr.: *To be nominated*) Flockhart	Emeryson-Climax	1475

24

Grid Positions

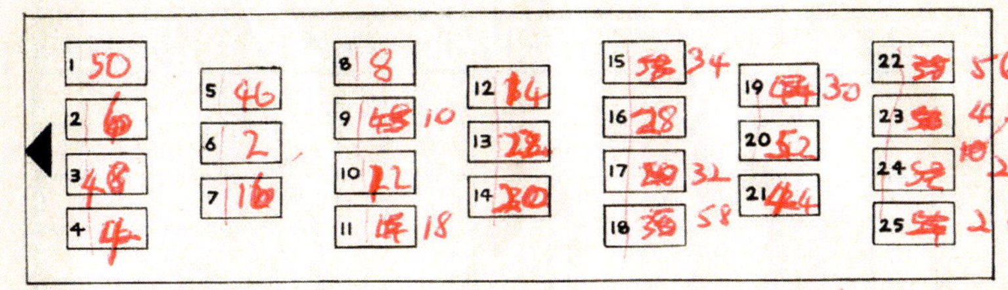

Results

1st 48. 4th 2

2nd 50 5th 12

3rd 4 6th 28.

Winner's Time ....

Speed 91.82 m.p.h.

Fastest Lap :

Car No. 50.

Time 1.42.6 Speed 92.98

Lap Chart on Pages 26 & 27

25

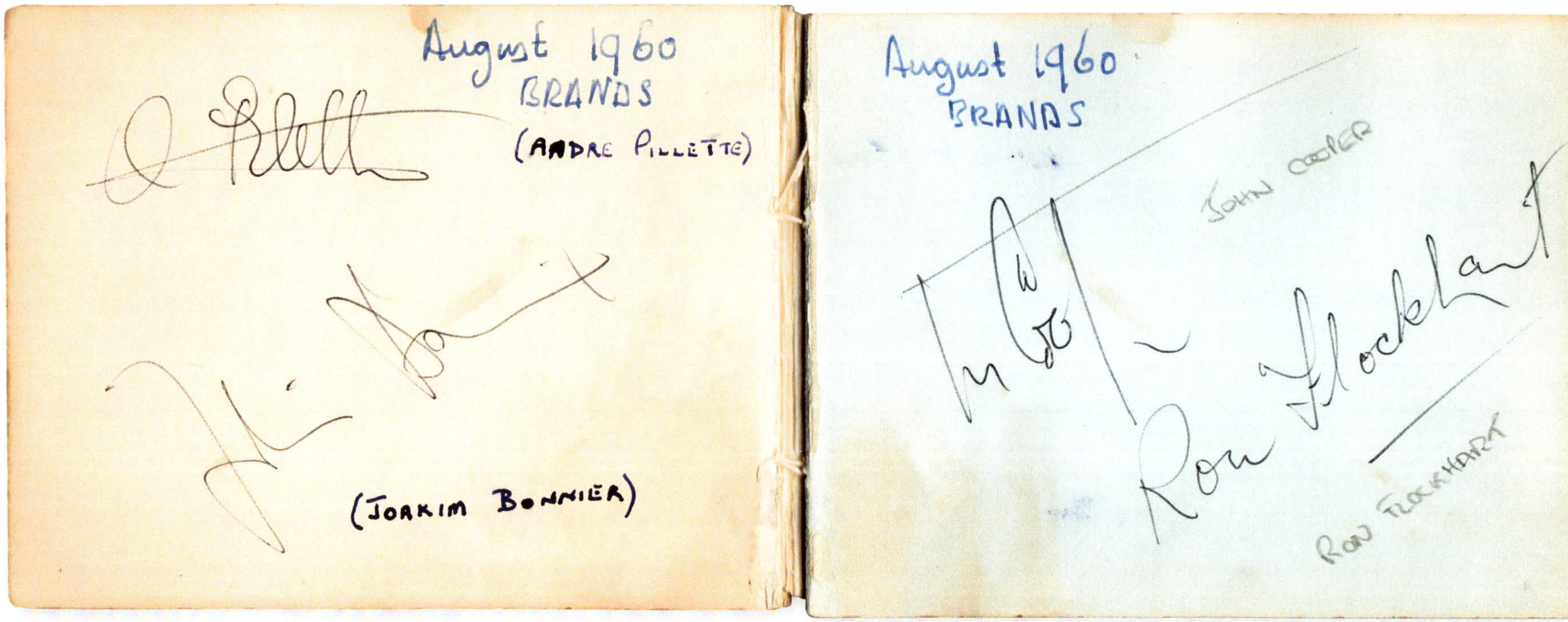

Andre Pilette

Andre's father Theodore raced to fifth place in the 1912 Indianapolis 500, his son Teddy was twice the European Formula 5000 Champion. Andre scored top six finishes in his home Belgian GP at Spa in 1951 in the Ecurie Belgique Talbot-Lago, for the Gordini factory team in 1954 and guest-driving for Ferrari in 1956. Eight years later he made his final F1 appearance in the Sirocco-BRM aged 45. He finished second at Le Mans in 1960 alongside Ricardo Rodriguez in a Ferrari and established a successful racing school at Zolder. ARM

Jo Bonnier

The bearded Jo Bonnier was not only the first Swede to compete in a Grand Prix, he was the first to win one, when he took victory for BRM in the 1959 Dutch GP. He also raced for Maserati, Porsche and Rob Walker. From a wealthy family, Bonnier was an Oxford graduate and from 1966 ran his own Formula 1 Cooper-Maserati and then sportscars - usually Lolas. In such a car – a T280 – he lost his life in the 1972 Le Mans 24 Hrs. ARM

Jo Bonnier, Porsche 718

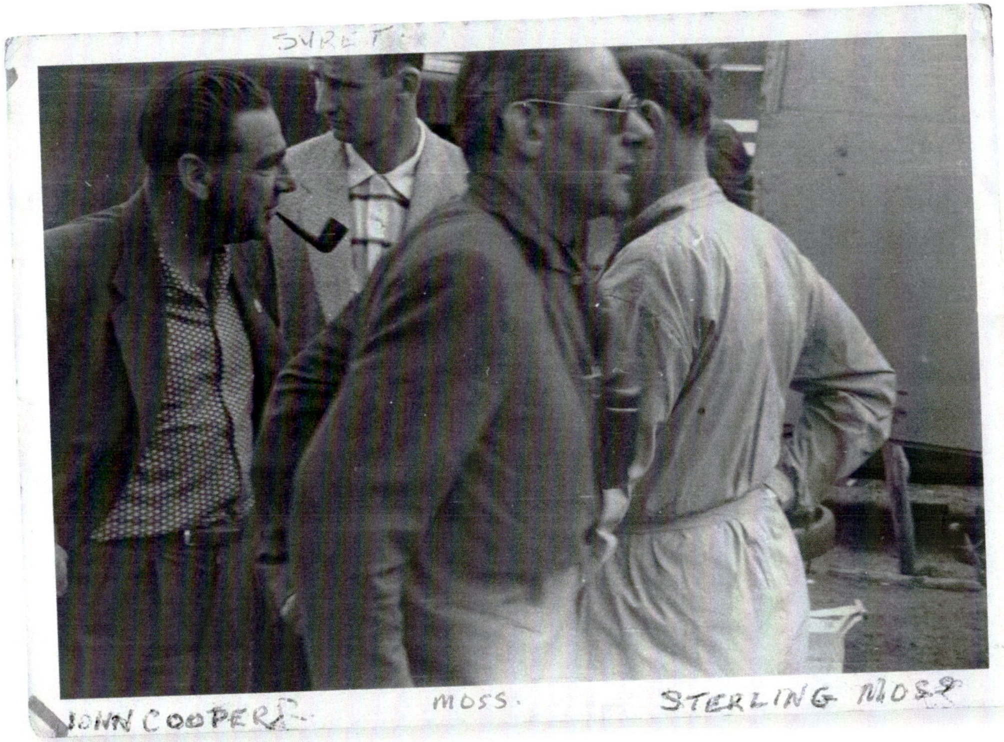

Pipe smoking John Cooper is on the left, Alfred Moss in the foreground (Charlie's hand-written caption suggests that it is him). His son Stirling (note hand-written spelling!) is on the right.

John Cooper

Surrey-based John Cooper was a pioneer and innovator and the Cooper Car Company he ran with his father Charles which was, for a while, the world's largest racing car manufacturer. Starting with their successful 500 cc F3 machines, they revolutionised the design of post-war racing cars by going rear-engined. They were successful at every level and Coopers won the World Championship in 1959 and 1960. Tasked by BMC to develop a high performance Mini they had further success and the name lives on today with the latest, rather larger, Minis built by BMW. ARM

Ron Flockhart

The Scot Ron Flockhart participated in 14 Grands Prix over a period of six seasons racing for everyone from Prince Bira to BRM and Team Lotus. But he was best known as a sportscar driver and won Le Mans in the Ecurie Ecosse Jaguar in both 1956 and 1957. Flockhart was killed when his WW2 Mustang aircraft crashed during a record attempt in Australia in 1962 ARM.

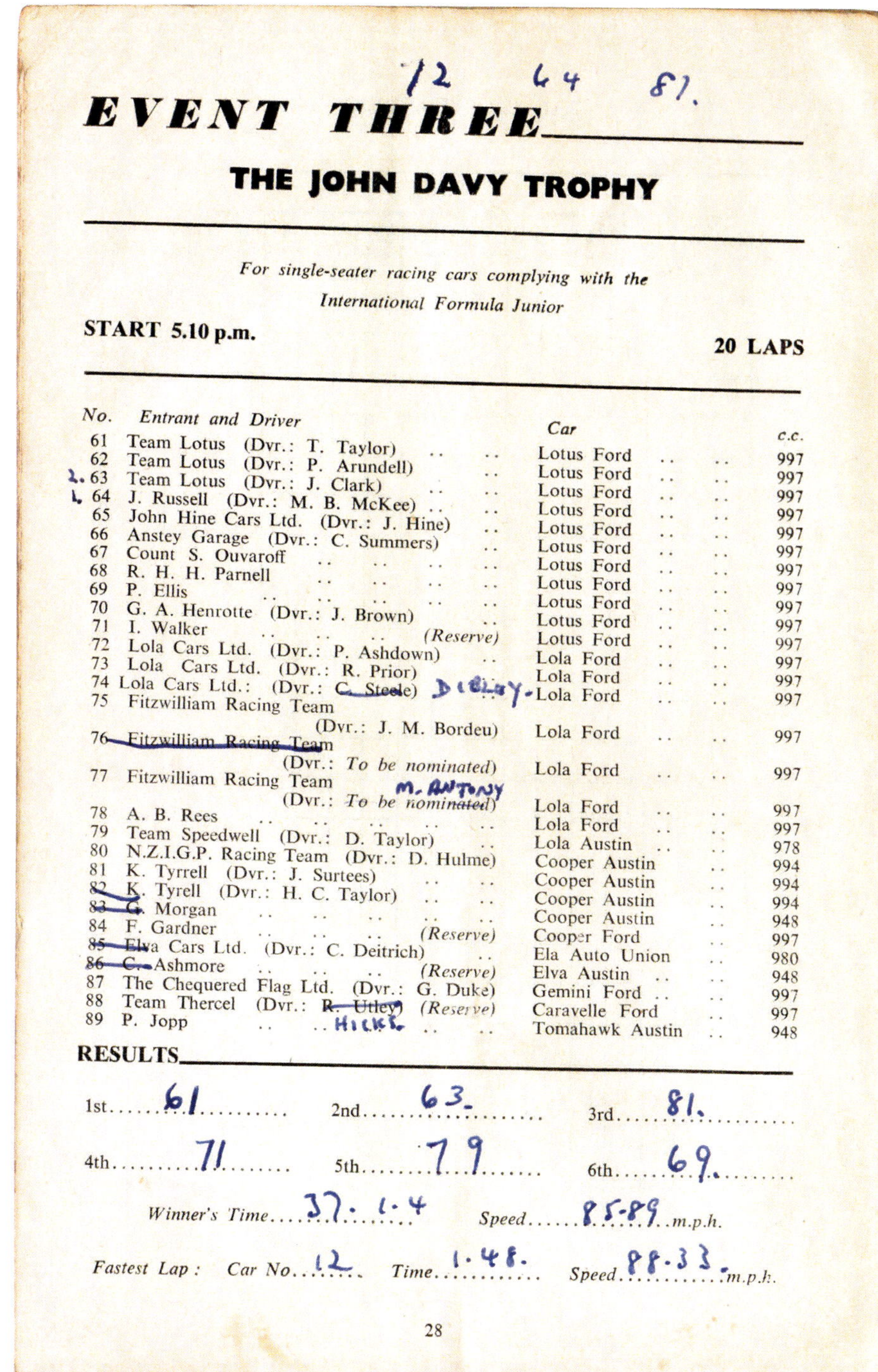

EVENT THREE

THE JOHN DAVY TROPHY

For single-seater racing cars complying with the International Formula Junior

START 5.10 p.m. **20 LAPS**

No.	Entrant and Driver	Car	c.c.
61	Team Lotus (Dvr.: T. Taylor)	Lotus Ford	997
62	Team Lotus (Dvr.: P. Arundell)	Lotus Ford	997
63	Team Lotus (Dvr.: J. Clark)	Lotus Ford	997
64	J. Russell (Dvr.: M. B. McKee)	Lotus Ford	997
65	John Hine Cars Ltd. (Dvr.: J. Hine)	Lotus Ford	997
66	Anstey Garage (Dvr.: C. Summers)	Lotus Ford	997
67	Count S. Ouvaroff	Lotus Ford	997
68	R. H. H. Parnell	Lotus Ford	997
69	P. Ellis	Lotus Ford	997
70	G. A. Henrotte (Dvr.: J. Brown)	Lotus Ford	997
71	I. Walker *(Reserve)*	Lotus Ford	997
72	Lola Cars Ltd. (Dvr.: P. Ashdown)	Lola Ford	997
73	Lola Cars Ltd. (Dvr.: R. Prior)	Lola Ford	997
74	Lola Cars Ltd.: (Dvr.: C. Steele)	Lola Ford	997
75	Fitzwilliam Racing Team (Dvr.: J. M. Bordeu)	Lola Ford	997
76	Fitzwilliam Racing Team (Dvr.: *To be nominated*)	Lola Ford	997
77	Fitzwilliam Racing Team (Dvr.: *To be nominated*)	Lola Ford	997
78	A. B. Rees	Lola Ford	997
79	Team Speedwell (Dvr.: D. Taylor)	Lola Austin	978
80	N.Z.I.G.P. Racing Team (Dvr.: D. Hulme)	Cooper Austin	994
81	K. Tyrrell (Dvr.: J. Surtees)	Cooper Austin	994
82	K. Tyrell (Dvr.: H. C. Taylor)	Cooper Austin	994
83	G. Morgan	Cooper Austin	948
84	F. Gardner *(Reserve)*	Cooper Ford	997
85	Elva Cars Ltd. (Dvr.: C. Deitrich)	Ela Auto Union	980
86	C. Ashmore *(Reserve)*	Elva Austin	948
87	The Chequered Flag Ltd. (Dvr.: G. Duke)	Gemini Ford	997
88	Team Thercel (Dvr.: R. Utley) *(Reserve)*	Caravelle Ford	997
89	P. Jopp	Tomahawk Austin	948

RESULTS

1st........61.......... 2nd........63.......... 3rd........81..........

4th........71.......... 5th........79.......... 6th........69..........

Winner's Time....37.1.4.... *Speed*....85.89....*m.p.h.*

Fastest Lap: Car No.....12.... *Time*....1.48.... *Speed*....88.33....*m.p.h.*

28

Entries for the Formula Junior race include three future F1 World Champions - Clark, Hulme and Surtees and five time motorcycle World Champion Geoff Duke.

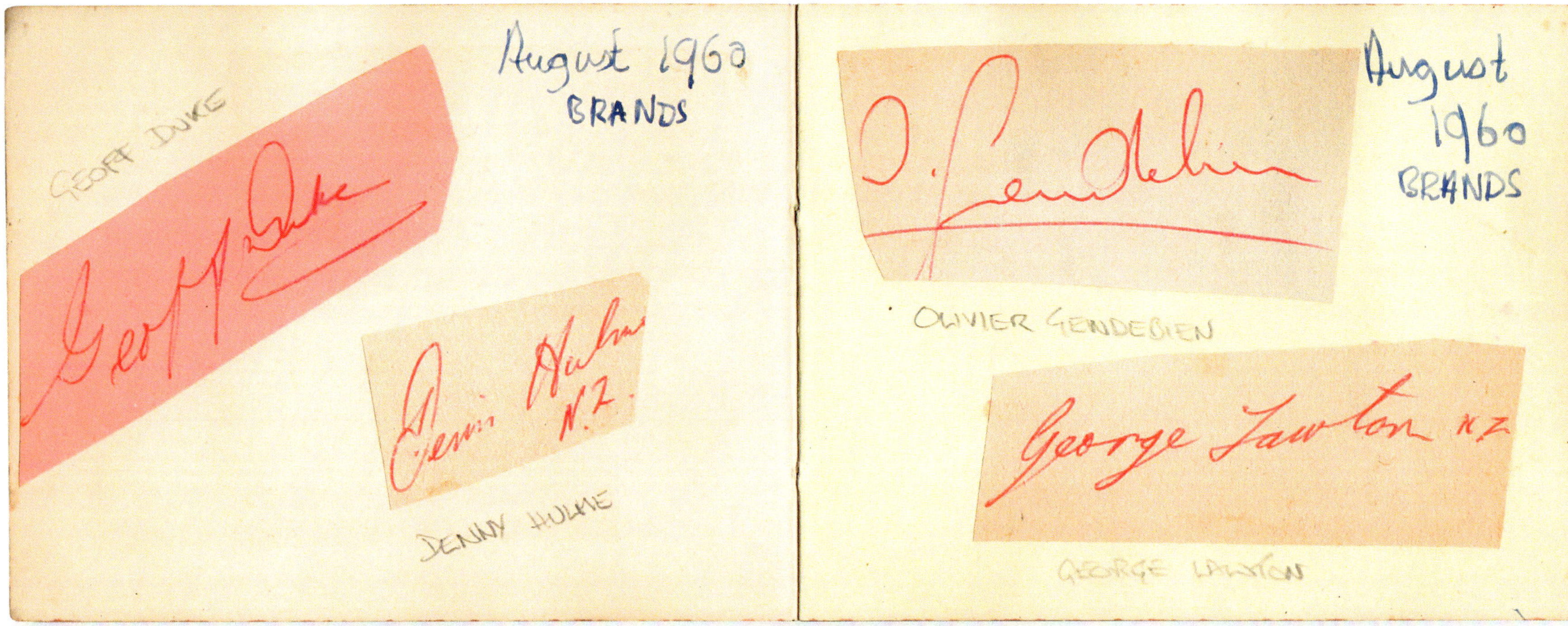

Not only had I forgotten to take my autoghraph book, but also had to borrow a red biro! All the autographs obtained on this day survived to be stuck into my book later.

Geoff Duke

Geoff Duke was Britain's best known motorcycle racer in the 1950s carving his reputation at the Isle of Man TT races around the dangerous course, winning nine times. He also won five World Championships in both the 350 and 500cc categories. He raced cars after he was suspended from bike racing after a riders strike. He drove for the Aston Martin sports car team and briefly in Formula 1 in a non-championship race in Sweden. ARM

Geoff Duke, 500cc Gilera, Isle of Man Senior TT, 1955

Denny Hulme

This tough New Zealander had the nickname "The Bear" and was the son of a Victoria Cross winner. He was born on a tobacco farm where he learned to drive a truck at the age of 6. He won a driver to Europe award and early success quickly saw him joining Jack Brabham's team initially winning in Formula Junior and Formula 2.

He made his Grand Prix debut in 1965 for Brabham and won the World Championship for them two years later. But in 1968 he jumped ship and joined his fellow Kiwi Bruce McLaren and spent seven years racing for the team winning six GPs for them. He won many more in the Can-Am series. He raced four times at the Indianapolis 500 twice finishing fourth. Later he raced trucks and touring cars and died from a heart attack during the 1992 Bathurst 1000. ARM

Olivier Gendebien, Ferrari TR59, Nürburgring*1000kms, 1959*

Olivier Gendebien

Although he raced occasionally in Formula 1, this Belgian was far better known for his exploits in sportscars. He won the World Sportscar Championship and the Le Mans 24 Hours in 1958 for Ferrari. He retired the following year but then won for the next three years for the Scuderia. He also won the Targa Florio three times, the Sebring 12 Hours three times, the Reims 12 Hours twice and the Nürburgring 1000 Kms once. After his fourth Le Mans win he retired to concentrate on business. ARM

Denny Hulme, Brabham Repco BT24, German GP, 1967

George Lawton

A true talent, New Zealander George, often known as Joe, had a Formula 1 contract in his pocket when he was killed at Roskildering in Denmark. His death left an opening for his friend and fellow Kiwi Denny Hulme. ARM

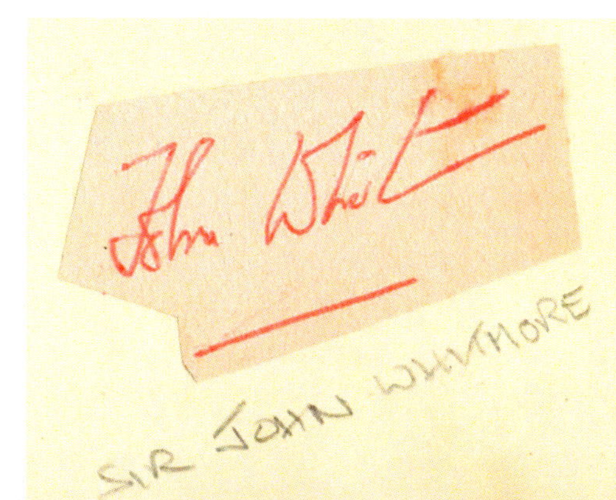

Sir John Whitmore

Old Etonian Sir John Whitmore was a hereditary baronet who was a leading saloon and sportscar racer in the 1960s. He raced factory Lotus, Healey and then Ford GT40s at Le Mans. He won the British Saloon Car Championship in a Don Moore Mini and later competed in a factory Lotus Cortina and Ford Falcon Sprint and was twice a category winner in the European Touring Car Championship. He also raced Alan Mann's Cobras to great effect. He later made a comeback in Historic events winning in his Lotus Cortina. He is became a successful performance coach with a best-selling book. ARM .

As well as racing in F1 for Lotus, John Surtees was still winning World Championships on bikes in 1960. Here he is winning the 1960 Isle of Man TT on a 500cc MV Augusta.

A Modest Man

I got to know John Surtees through kart racing as his son Henry and my son Sam raced at the same race meetings. It says something about the man that years later he didn't hesitate to help Sam with the relevant aspects of his university dissertation on Motorsport Management.

We also worked together on a fund-raising project (see page 70) which entailed me painting his 1966 Can Am winning Lola T70 and John signing the prints of it. We met at the Goodwood Festival of Speed to discuss the project. John, as always was a very busy man and was just about to blast up the hill on an MV Augusta. However, he was happy to talk to me "but be quick!"

The meeting room was the back of a white transit-like van. While we discussed the project John stripped off to his underpants and then put on his motorcycle leathers in front of me before saying goodbye and rushing off to his awaiting machine.

Not many World Champions are that modest. John Surtees, who put so much back into motorsport most certainly was. MT

John Surtees

When a short-trousered young Martin Tomlinson collected John Surtees' autograph little could he have imagined that their sons would race karts together and they would join forces to work on a charity project!

John Surtees is, of course, the only man to have the World Championship on both two and four wheels. John was the son of a South London motorcycle dealer and started his racing at aged 15. In 1956 aged 21 he won his first of seven motorcycle titles riding Italian MV Agustas.

While others struggled to translate their talent onto four wheels John did so effortlessly and in 1964 won the World Championship for Ferrari. He later drove for Honda, BRM and McLaren before becoming a Formula 1 constructor and team owner and also building cars for several other high-profile categories. His talented son Henry was killed in a freak racing accident while "Big John" died aged 83. ARM

The Belgian GP, Spa, 12 June 1966 was possibly John Surtees' 'day of days.' In his last F1 race for Ferrari, he annihilated the opposition in the atrocious wet conditions which had caught out eight drivers in first lap accidents. Here, he is followed by Jochen Rindt (Cooper-Maserati) who was the only un-lapped driver, finishing 43 seconds behind the flying Surtees. MT

6
19

FULL SUTTON

In the immediate post-war years, if you lived on the Continent and wanted to organise a race meeting, it was easy. You simply closed a few roads, placed straw bales in front of some of the telegraph poles, trees and buildings which lined the circuit. Spectators watched from the edge of the circuit, protected by nothing more than a paling fence, a length of rope, straw bales, a hedge or even barbed wire. The lucky ones could watch from the relative safety of their local bar. Circuit safety wasn't a consideration for spectators or drivers.

In Britain racing on public roads was illegal with the exceptions of The Isle of Man, Northern Ireland and the Channel Islands. So organising a race meeting like our European neighbours wasn't an option in mainland Britain.

However, what Britain did have after the war was dozens of redundant airfields with concrete runways. With strategically placed straw bales these made perfectly good, but mainly flat and featureless race circuits. Owing to the amount of available space spectators were further back from the circuit than those in Europe though with the same rudimentary safety precautions. A double-decker bus made a perfect race control.

Enthusiast-run clubs such as the Northern section of the British Racing and Sports Car Club organised many such meetings on airfields in Yorkshire like Rufforth, Elvington, and Linton-on-Ouse. On 5th April 1958 they organised the first meeting at Full Sutton airfield. MT

British Racing & Sports Car Club

Official

Rufforth

Whit Saturday, 4th June

1960

FULL SUTTON CIRCUIT

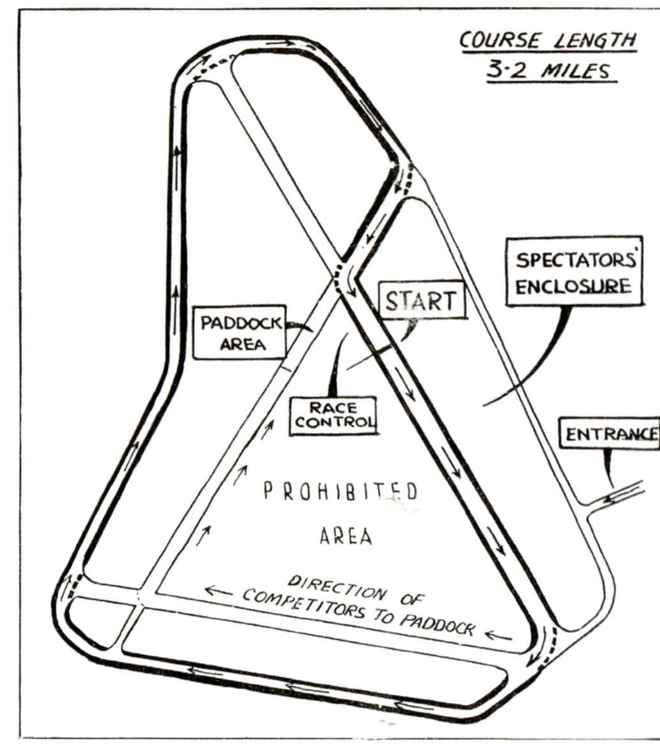

By courtesy of the Yorkshire Evening Post

WARNING !
MOTOR RACING IS DANGEROUS

You are present at this meeting entirely at your own risk, and you are admitted subject to the conditions that all persons having connection with the promotion and organisation or conduct of this meeting including the Owners of the land and Drivers and Owners of the vehicles, are absolved from all liability in respect of personal injury whether fatal or otherwise to you, or damage to your property howsoever caused.

B.R.S.C.C.

BRITISH RACING & SPORTS CAR CLUB

R.A.C. COMP. NO. R. 277

Motor Race Meeting

Full Sutton *near* York

SATURDAY 5th April 1958 at 1.30 p.m.

PROGRAMME and donation to Club **1/-**

(Dogs not admitted)

The promoters reserve the right of admission to the circuit. Spectators are requested to keep off all farm land.

PROGRAMME

EVENT 6. 3.45 p.m.

8 Lap Scratch Race for Racing and Sports Racing Cars of Unlimited Capacity. Grid Start.

No.	*Driver*	*Car*	*c.c. Capacity*	
48.	M. J. L. BROOK	Austin Healey 100	2639 c.c.	Huddersfield
49.	D. BROOK	Austin Healey 100	2639 c.c.	Huddersfield
50.	K. J. COFFEY	Jaguar S.S.100	3500 c.c.	Flixton
56.	D. G. MILK	Jaguar S.S.100	3485 c.c.	Cheadle
59.	I. H. S. SMITH (Entrant Team Triples)	A.C. Bristol	1971 c.c.	Keighley
61.	C. R. HANSON (Entrant Team Triples)	Austin Healey 100.S.	2660 c.c.	Leeds
62.	A. G. M. KELLETT (Entrant Team Triples)	Austin Healey 100.S.	2660 c.c.	Leeds
63.	P. H. SUTCLIFFE (Entrant Team Triples)	Frazer Nash Le Mans	1971 c.c.	Leeds
64.	J. CLARK (Entrant Border Reivers)	Porsche Super	1600 c.c.	Berwickshire
71.	J. C. BRIERLEY	Victoria Climax	1097 c.c.	Rochdale
73.	L. I. BRAMLEY	Lotus Climax Mk. XI	1097 c.c.	Northallerton
74.	B. J. COX	Elva M.G.	1467 c.c.	Stockport
75.	T. T. CANDLISH	Lotus Climax Mk. VI	1097 c.c.	Hartlepool
77.	B. HARPIN	Lotus Climax Mk. XI	1097 c.c.	Liversedge
78.	J. HIGHAM	Lotus Climax Mk. XI	1215 c.c.	Leeds
79.	D. HOWARD	Cooper Climax	1098 c.c.	Bridlington
82.	C. MEEK	Lotus Connought	1472 c.c.	Leeds
83.	E. J. B. MITCHELL	Lotus Ford	1172 c.c.	Huddersfield
84.	J. L. ROMANES	Lotus Climax Mk. XI	1097 c.c.	Edinburgh
85.	J. STEELE	Lotus Climax Mk. XI	1097 c.c.	Edinburgh
89.	J. BURGESS	Lotus Climax Mk. XI	1097 c.c.	Middlesbrough
92.	J. A. SOMERVAIL (Entrant Border Reivers)	Jaguar D. Type	3442 c.c.	Berwickshire
93.	A. ENSOLL	Jaguar C. Type	3442 c.c.	Middlesbrough
94.	F. ELLIOTT	Lister Bristol	1971 c.c.	Middlesbrough
95.	C. MURRAY	Cooper Jaguar	3442 c.c.	Fleetwood
90.	E. J. ALLEN	Lotus Mk. XI	1098 c.c.	Southport
91.	J. BLUMER	Lotus Climax Mk. IX	1089 c.c.	Middlesbrough
96.	J. BERRY	E.R.A. Special	1960 c.c.	Rochdale

1st.................... 2nd.................... 3rd....................

Winner's Speed.................... Fastest Lap Car No.................... speed....................

Car 92, the Border Reivers D Type Jaguar, was originally entered for Jimmy Somervail to drive. However, he was unable make it that weekend and so Jim Clark drove it instead.

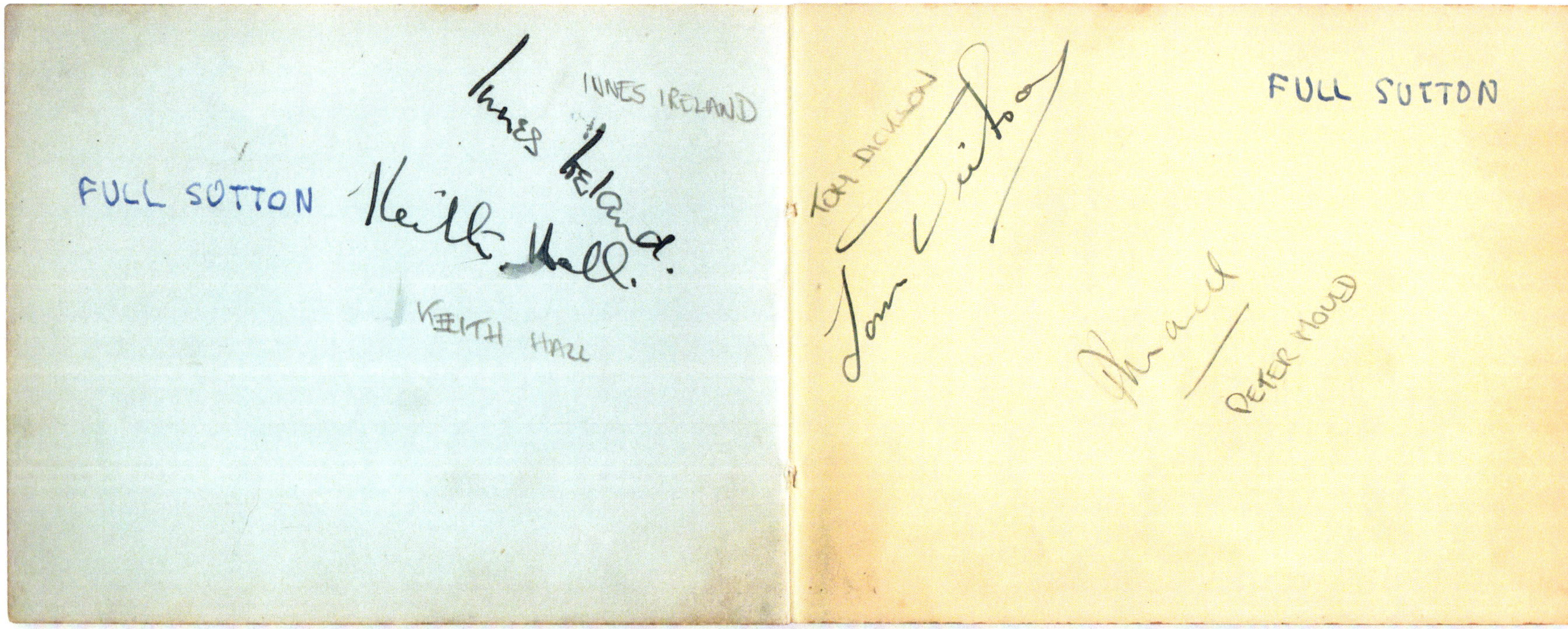

Innes Ireland

A commissioned officer in the Parachute Regiment, Ireland took up racing after he was he was de-mobbed and quickly established himself not only as a fast and fearless racer but also one of the sport's great characters. Sportscar success was followed by a drive for Team Lotus in Formula 1. He started a turbulent 1961 with a bad crash at Monaco but recovered from his injuries to give Colin Chapman's Team Lotus their first Grand Prix win at the US Grand Prix at Watkins Glen.

His reward was the sack and he moved on to drive for privateer teams for the next five years but was never on the podium again except in some non-championship races. But there were sportscar successes and he moved on first to a life as motor racing journalist and then skippered fishing trawlers. He died of cancer aged 63. His daughter races occasionally. ARM

Innes Ireland (pre chequered helmet days), Lotus XI, Full Sutton, 1958

Keith Hall

A front-running 500cc Formula 3 driver in the 1950s, Hall switched to sportscars, driving for such top teams as Border Reivers and Team Lotus. In 1957 in a Lotus XI fitted with a tiny 750cc Climax engine, he won the Index of Performance at Le Mans and his class together with team mate Cliff Allison. He then moved up to Formula 2 with Lotus but decided to retire at the end of 1958. He died in 2017 at the age of 87. ARM

Tom Dickson

Perth garage group owner Tom Dickson didn't look like a racing driver, just 5ft 2in tall with thick rimless glasses but in the 50s/60s he was considered one of Scotland's top racers. He competed at Le Mans for Team Lotus and Ecurie Ecosse and was British Sportscar Champion in 1962. ARM

"...we were just a group of enthusiasts in those days"

The Full Sutton meeting on Saturday 5 April saw a six race programme. The main event of the day the 'Yorkshire Evening Post Trophy' was a 12 lap Formula Libre race. Among the starters was a relatively unknown Scot called Jim Clark. Clark had driven the Border Reivers D Type Jaguar down the A1 from Berwick on Tweed to York the previous night because the team's transporter had broken down. This was his first experience of driving a powerful racing car and he did so in driving snowstorm conditions on a public road. Clark had obviously got the hang of it as he won and set fastest lap in the main event.

To oversee the running of the meeting was RAC's Head of Motorsport, Dean Delamont. Part of his official remit was to travel as passenger in the course car. This entailed doing a lap of the circuit before each race to ensure that the it was clear, safe and ready for the race. All went to plan until the F3 event. The course car was only half way round the lap when the unmistakable roar of 500cc racing engines, getting louder and louder, could be heard coming from behind it. The officials turned to see the entire F3 field rapidly bearing down on them. The course car swerved off the track to avoid getting involved in the race, just as the field tore past! It seems that a nervous starter had inadvertently dropped the flag somewhat prematurely.

At the end of the day the race officials retired to the local pub to review the days' events. Unfortunately calculations in respect of Clark's fastest lap were made after a few pints and initially showed an average speed in excess of 120 mph. This was significant news and was quickly phoned through to the motoring press. That Full Sutton was now the fastest circuit in the country at that time resulted in even more pints being consumed. Fortunately, when the alcohol and euphoria wore off the true figure of 103.8mph* was established before the the news had gone to print!

As Maurice recently explained "You have to understand, we were just a group of enthusiasts in those days" MT

*This was nevertheless the fastest lap achieved by a sports car on a British circuit.

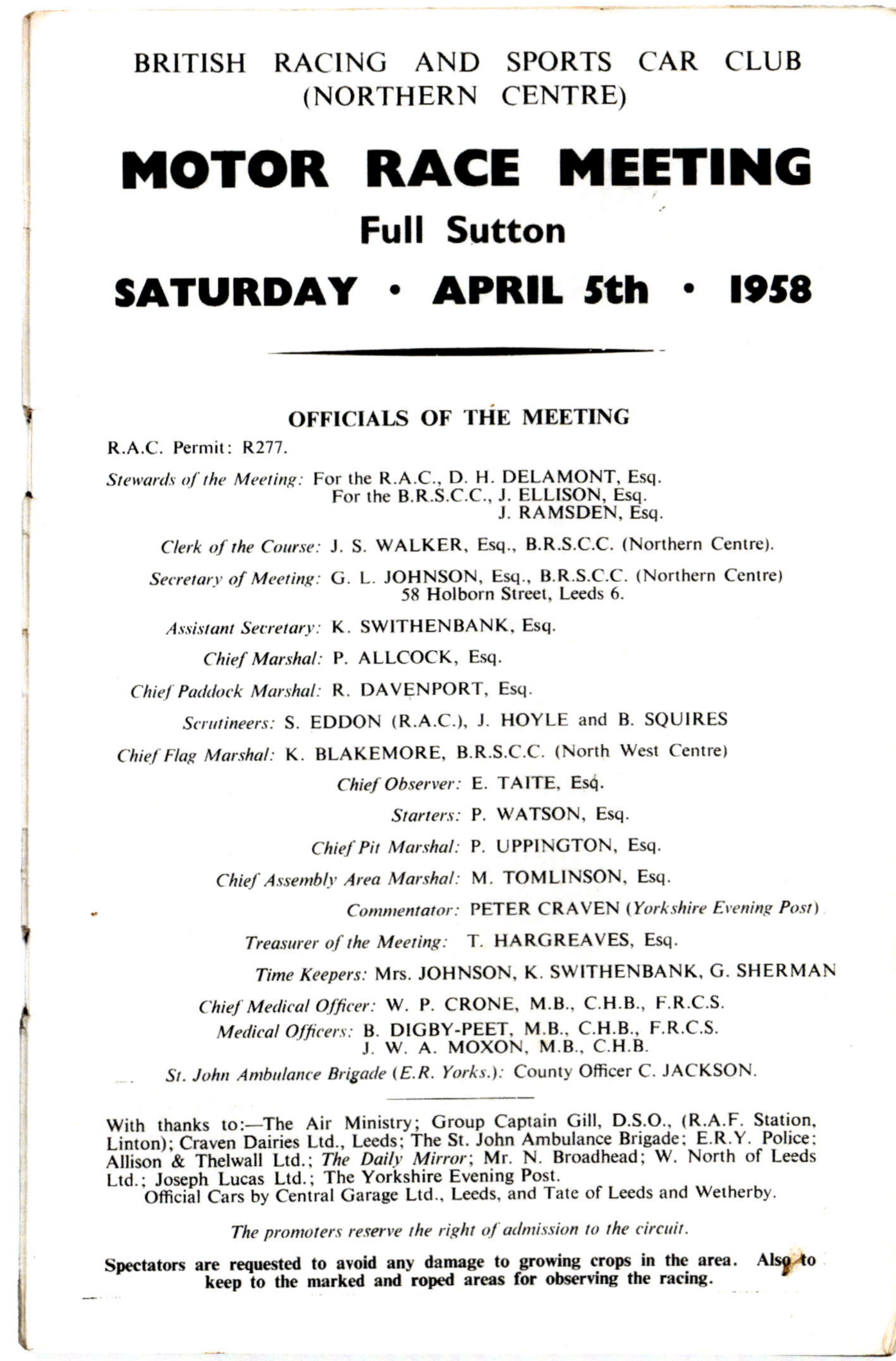
BRITISH RACING AND SPORTS CAR CLUB
(NORTHERN CENTRE)

MOTOR RACE MEETING

Full Sutton

SATURDAY • APRIL 5th • 1958

OFFICIALS OF THE MEETING

R.A.C. Permit: R277.

Stewards of the Meeting: For the R.A.C., D. H. DELAMONT, Esq.
For the B.R.S.C.C., J. ELLISON, Esq.
J. RAMSDEN, Esq.

Clerk of the Course: J. S. WALKER, Esq., B.R.S.C.C. (Northern Centre).

Secretary of Meeting: G. L. JOHNSON, Esq., B.R.S.C.C. (Northern Centre)
58 Holborn Street, Leeds 6.

Assistant Secretary: K. SWITHENBANK, Esq.

Chief Marshal: P. ALLCOCK, Esq.

Chief Paddock Marshal: R. DAVENPORT, Esq.

Scrutineers: S. EDDON (R.A.C.), J. HOYLE and B. SQUIRES

Chief Flag Marshal: K. BLAKEMORE, B.R.S.C.C. (North West Centre)

Chief Observer: E. TAITE, Esq.

Starters: P. WATSON, Esq.

Chief Pit Marshal: P. UPPINGTON, Esq.

Chief Assembly Area Marshal: M. TOMLINSON, Esq.

Commentator: PETER CRAVEN (*Yorkshire Evening Post*)

Treasurer of the Meeting: T. HARGREAVES, Esq.

Time Keepers: Mrs. JOHNSON, K. SWITHENBANK, G. SHERMAN

Chief Medical Officer: W. P. CRONE, M.B., C.H.B., F.R.C.S.

Medical Officers: B. DIGBY-PEET, M.B., C.H.B., F.R.C.S.
J. W. A. MOXON, M.B., C.H.B.

St. John Ambulance Brigade (E.R. Yorks.): County Officer C. JACKSON.

With thanks to:—The Air Ministry; Group Captain Gill, D.S.O., (R.A.F. Station, Linton); Craven Dairies Ltd., Leeds; The St. John Ambulance Brigade; E.R.Y. Police; Allison & Thelwall Ltd.; *The Daily Mirror*; Mr. N. Broadhead; W. North of Leeds Ltd.; Joseph Lucas Ltd.; The Yorkshire Evening Post.
Official Cars by Central Garage Ltd., Leeds, and Tate of Leeds and Wetherby.

The promoters reserve the right of admission to the circuit.

Spectators are requested to avoid any damage to growing crops in the area. Also to keep to the marked and roped areas for observing the racing.

The guilty parties are among those listed above.
That includes a certain Chief Assembly Area Marshal 'M. Tomlinson, Esq.'!

AINTREE

I don't know why the sound of a racing engine puts a smile on my face, but it does! Those who have heard the sound of a V16 BRM will know what I mean. I was fortunate enough to hear one and to see Peter Collins drive the works car to its last ever race win at Aintree in September 1955.

That was my first visit to to Aintree and many more followed over the next nine years. There's not the room to describe them all here and I suspect not a sufficiently good memory to do so even if there was! However, here are some of my memorable meetings at the circuit.

One of them was the International Aintree 200 F1 race in April 1956. Entries included BRMs for Hawthorn and Brooks, Connaughts for pole sitter, the incredible Archie Scott Brown and Parnell and Maserati 250Fs for winner Moss, Salvadori and Brabham.

The 1964 Aintree 200. Brabham duelled for most of the race with Clark who crashed late in the race leaving the win to 'Black Jack'. In the sports car race Bruce McLaren won in his 3.5 litre Cooper Oldsmobile, forerunner of McLaren's eponymous Can-Am cars.

And then there were the Grands Prix of 1961 and 1962. MT.

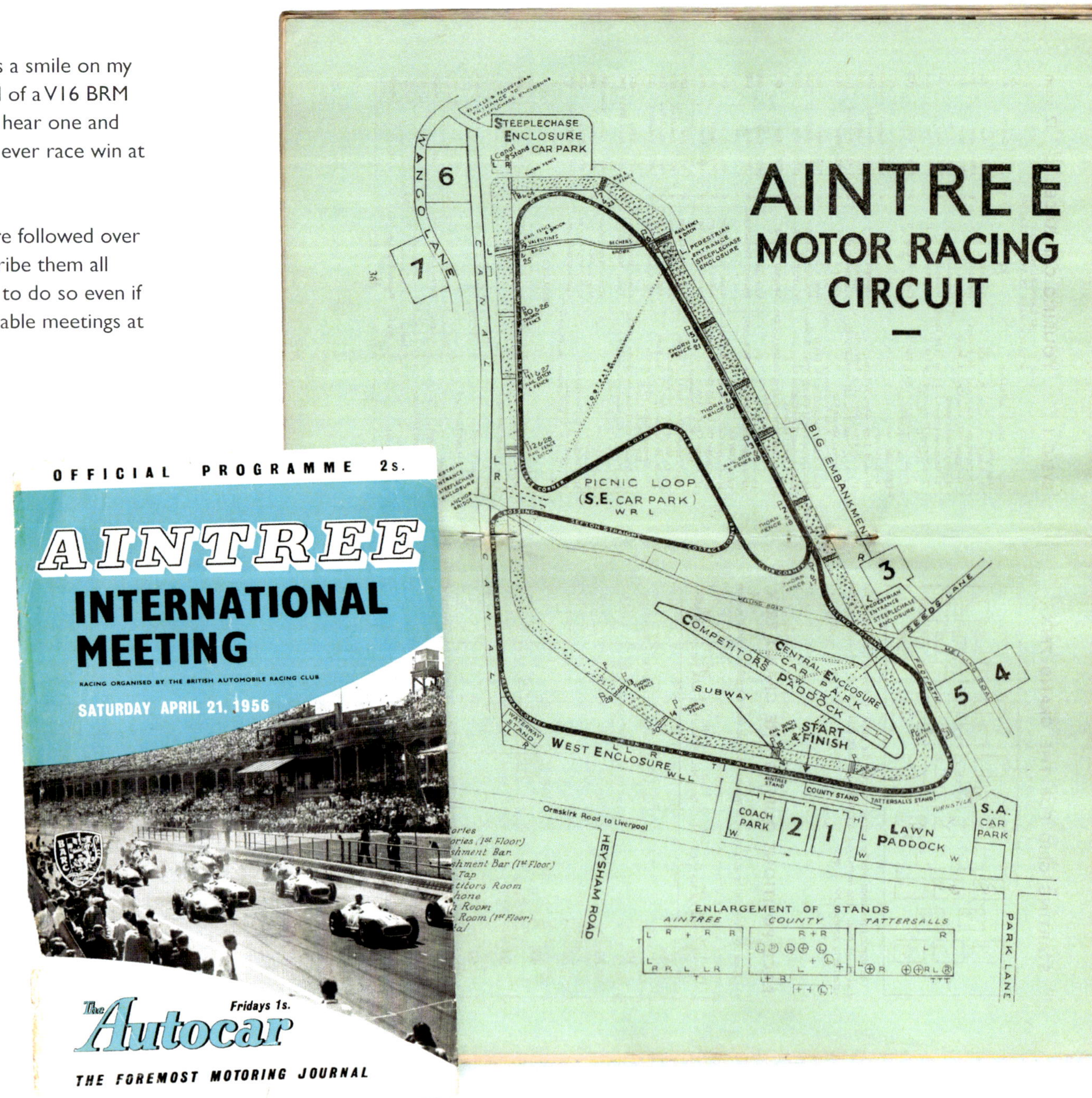

EVENT 2 **BRITISH GRAND PRIX** 2.30 p.m.

(75 LAPS—225 MILES)

Scratch race for Formula I cars

No.	*Car*	*Driver*	*Nationality*	*Entrant*
2	FERRARI	P. Hill	American	*S.E.F.A.C. Ferrari*
4	FERRARI	W. von Trips	German	*S.E.F.A.C. Ferrari*
6	FERRARI	R. Ginther	American	*S.E.F.A.C. Ferrari*
8	PORSCHE	J. Bonnier	Swedish	*Porsche System Engineering Ltd.*
10	PORSCHE	D. Gurney	American	*Porsche System Engineering Ltd.*
12	COOPER	J. Brabham	Australian	*Cooper Car Co. Ltd.*
14	COOPER	B. McLaren	New Zealand	*Cooper Car Co. Ltd.*
16	LOTUS	I. Ireland	British	*Team Lotus*
18	LOTUS	J. Clark	British	*Team Lotus*
20	B.R.M.	G. Hill	British	*Owen Racing Organisation*
22	B.R.M.	C. A. S. Brooks	British	*Owen Racing Organisation*
24	*Withdrawn*			
26	FERGUSON	J. E. G. Fairman	British	*Ferguson Research*
28	LOTUS	S. Moss	British	*R. R. C. Walker Racing Team*
30	LOTUS	H. C. Taylor	British	*U.D.T. Laystall Racing Team*
32	LOTUS	L. Bianchi	Belgian	*U.D.T. Laystall Racing Team*
34	COOPER	J. Surtees	British	*Yeoman Credit Racing Team*
36	COOPER	R. Salvadori	British	*Yeoman Credit Racing Team*
38	LOTUS	R. H. H. Parnell	British	*R. H. H. Parnell*
40	LOTUS	G. Ashmore	British	*G. Ashmore*
42	COOPER	M. Gregory	American	*Camoradi International*
44	LOTUS	I. Burgess	British	*Camoradi International*
46	COOPER	J. Lewis	British	*H. & L. Motors Ltd.*
48	LOTUS	T. Marsh	British	*T. Marsh*
50	LOTUS	T. Maggs	South African	*Mrs. L. Bryden-Brown*
52	LOTUS	W. Seidel	German	*Scuderia Colonia*
54	GILBY	K. A. Greene	British	*Gilby Engineering Co. Ltd.*
56	PORSCHE	Count G. de Beaufort	Dutch	*Ecurie Maarsbergen*
58	FERRARI	G. Baghetti	Italian	*Scuderia Santambroeus*
60	COOPER-MASERATI	L. Bandini	Italian	*Scuderia Centro-Sud*
62	COOPER-MASERATI	M. Natili	Italian	*Scuderia Centro-Sud*

RESULT

1st......4...... 2nd......2...... 3rd......6...... 4th......12......

Winner's Speed................m.p.h. Fastest Lap : Car No...22...at........m.p.h.

39

5th 8 6th 36.

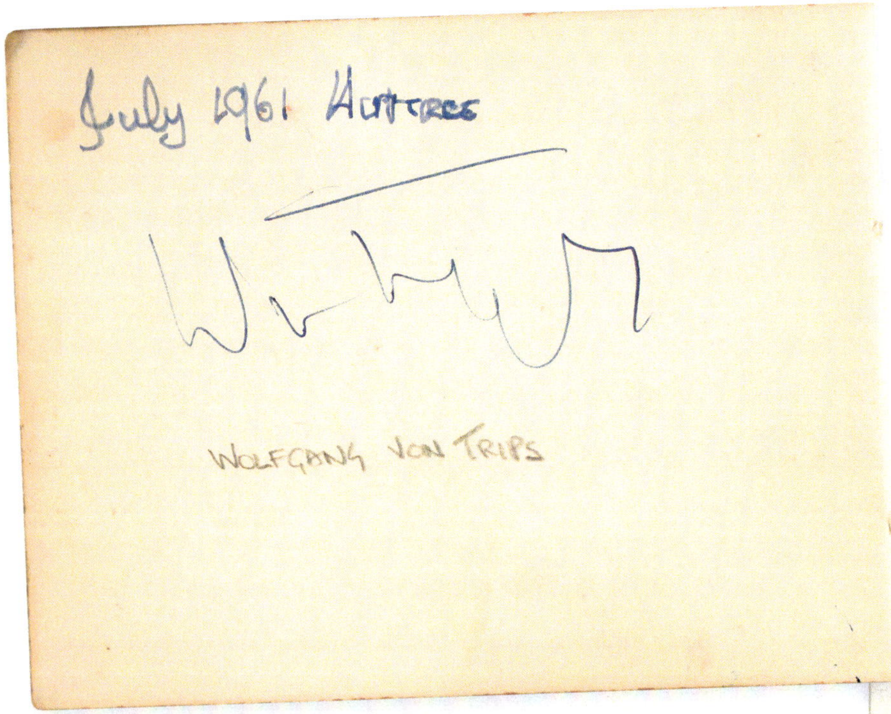

Wolfgang von Trips

Wolfgang Alexander Albert Eduard Maximillian Reichsgraf Berghe von Trips to give him his full name was a German who raced for Ferrari. He was the son of a noble Rhineland family. He died at the age of 34 when he crashed the sharknose 156 in the 1961 Italian GP at Monza whilst fighting for the World Championship.

He collided with Jim Clark's Lotus and the Ferrari tragically flew into the crowd. As well as von Trips, fifteen trackside spectators perished. At the time he was leading the title chase and a third place would have secured him the title. He would have become the first German to win it. It wasn't until Michael Schumacher's 1994 title that the country finally had a World Champion. The 1961 title went to von Trips' team mate Phil Hill who became the first of only two Americans to win the title. The iconic sharknose cars were "de-constructed" by Ferrari although some excellent replicas have subsequently been built.

The handsome Cologne-born racer, who had diabetes, initially had success in sports-car racing and Formula 2 racing before making his debut his Formula 1 in Argentina in 1957. Nicknamed "Taffy" by Mike Hawthorn who thought he looked Welsh, he won the prestigious Targa Florio in 1961 as well as taking wins at Zandvoort and then in the British GP at Aintree. ARM

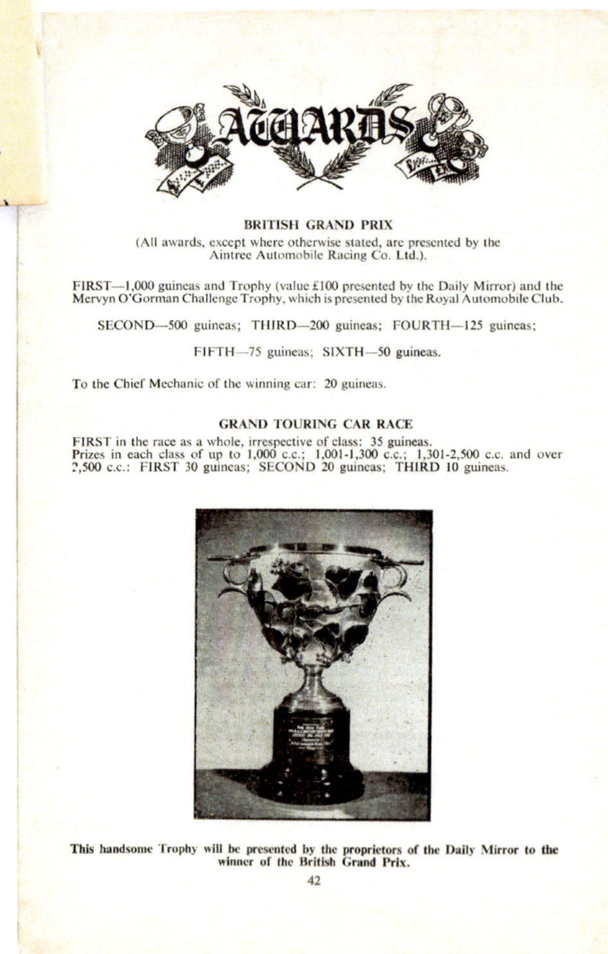

AWARDS

BRITISH GRAND PRIX

(All awards, except where otherwise stated, are presented by the Aintree Automobile Racing Co. Ltd.).

FIRST—1,000 guineas and Trophy (value £100 presented by the Daily Mirror) and the Mervyn O'Gorman Challenge Trophy, which is presented by the Royal Automobile Club.

SECOND—500 guineas; THIRD—200 guineas; FOURTH—125 guineas;

FIFTH—75 guineas; SIXTH—50 guineas.

To the Chief Mechanic of the winning car: 20 guineas.

GRAND TOURING CAR RACE

FIRST in the race as a whole, irrespective of class: 35 guineas.
Prizes in each class of up to 1,000 c.c.; 1,001-1,300 c.c.; 1,301-2,500 c.c. and over 2,500 c.c.: FIRST 30 guineas; SECOND 20 guineas; THIRD 10 guineas.

This handsome Trophy will be presented by the proprietors of the Daily Mirror to the winner of the British Grand Prix.

42

'Taffy' von Trips went home 1000 guineas to the good. The Ferrari Chief mechanic was 20 guineas better off, though he probably had to share it with the other mechanics.

Worth Waiting For

It didn't half rain at Aintree that day. We got soaked standing at the front of the Tattersall stands watching the day's racing. I can still remember von Trips raising both hands in a triumphant clinch, as boxers used to do, as he took the chequered flag.

After the race we went across the track to the paddock which was a cinder covered area behind the pits in those days. And there, standing with a small group of autograph hunters in his trenchcoat and Tyrolean-style hat was the winner of the British Grand Prix, Wolfgang von Trips. Undaunted I went over to join the small group to ask for his signature. However, there were looks of disappointment all round when he told us no he couldn't sign as he had to find his lost car keys first. But he did say, that if we wanted to wait he would come back once he had found them.

Well, we didn't expect him to return just to sign a few autograph books but thought we should at least wait for a while. To our amazement, a little while later he did return with his missing car keys and signed my book and those of the others. Wolfgang von Trips - a true gentleman!

On that same day I also managed to get the signatures of the other Ferrari drivers Phil Hill, Richie Ginther and Giancarlo Baghetti. MT

In a dominant display the 'Sharknose' Ferraris filled the first 3 places at the 1961 British GP.

Wolfgang 'Taffy' von Trips leads team mates Phil Hill and Richie Ginther through Tatts Corner. MT

THE MOTOR
The Autocar
CASTROL
AVON
BP

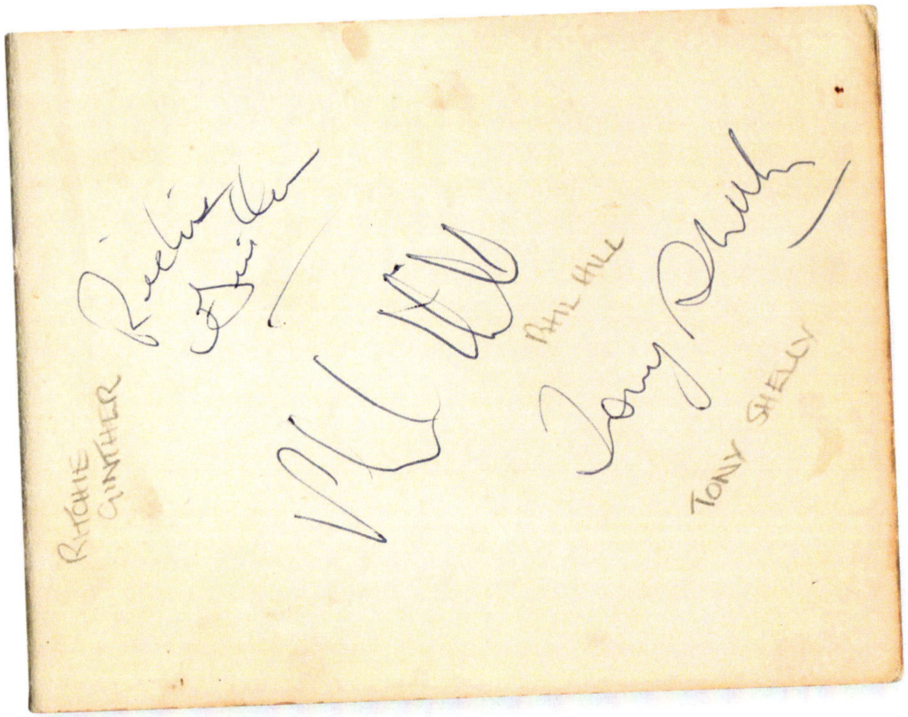

Richie Ginther

The Californian Richie Ginther impressed in sportscars before making his Grand Prix debut for Ferrari in the 1960 Monaco GP. After some solid results, including second at Monaco the following year, he switched to the BRM team in 1962. The following year he finished equal second to Graham Hill in the World Championship.

His reputation as a team player and excellent test and development driver earned him a place with the works Honda team in 1965. He famously gave them their first ever Formula 1 victory in the 1965 Mexican GP. But in 1967, after failing to qualify for the Indianapolis 500 and affected by the death of friend Lorenzo Bandini, he retired. He died from a heart attack in 1989, aged 59. ARM

Phil Hill

Philip Hill jnr wrote his name into the history books by becoming the first of the only two Americans ever to have won the World Championship, a feat he achieved for Ferrari in 1961. Although born in Miami, he was raised in Southern California but came to England to be a Jaguar trainee in 1949. He signed for Ferrari in 1956, first racing sportscar and was given his Grand Prix opportunity two years later in a privateer Maserati. Later that season Ferrari promoted him to the F1 team and he finished the season with two third places. His first Grand Prix win came in 1960 at the Italian GP at Monza. He won there again the following year and also at Spa – together with other top results he took the title.

A sophisticated and quietly-spoken man Hill also had tremendous success in sportscars, winning Le Mans for Ferrari on three occasions 1958, 1961 and 1962. Later he raced at Le Mans for Ford in the GT40 and the Chaparrals. He was a three-time winner of the Sebring 12 Hours and won the Daytona 24 Hours in 1964. He won his first ever race in an MGTC and his last in the Chaparral in the Brands Hatch BOAC 500 in 1967. He died aged 81. ARM

Tony Shelley

New Zealander Shelley was a race winner "down under" before heading to Europe where he raced Derbyshire oil man John Dalton's Lotus 18 in 1962 non-championship F1 races. A third at Goodwood marked him out as a coming man but at the end of the season he returned home where he raced for a couple of years before setting up a thriving car dealership network. ARM

Richie Ginther's greatest race, Ferrari 156, Monaco GP, 1961

Phil Hill's 1962 Le Mans winning Ferrari 330TR1/LM leading the McLaren / Hansgen Maserati Tipo 151 through the Esses. MT

MULTIGRADE
SUPERSHELL-IGA
SHELL
AVEC
6

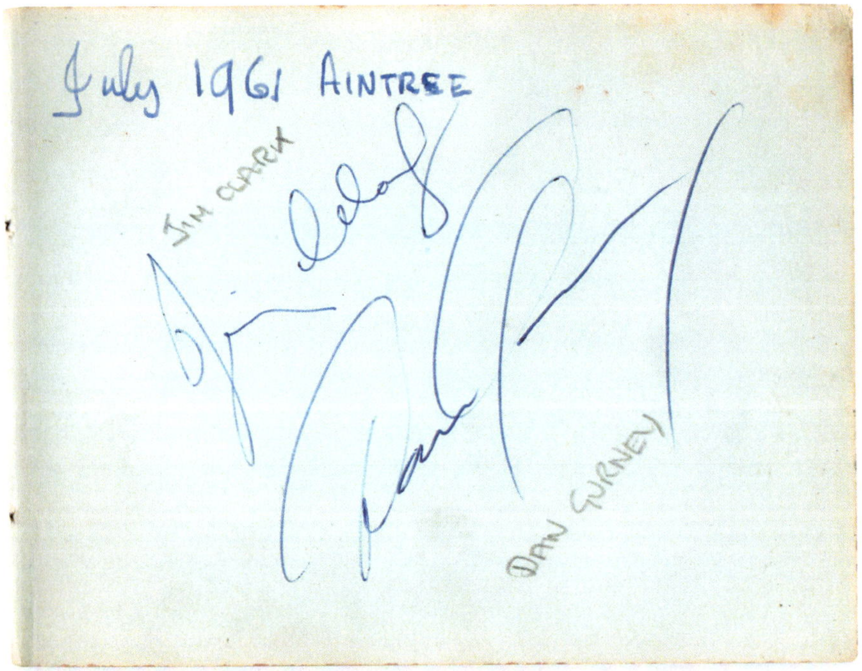

Dan Gurney

New York-born Daniel Sexton Gurney was a highly respected racing driver, race car constructor and team owner who won races not only at Formula 1 level but also in Indycar, NASCAR, Can-Am and Trans-Am. He is one of only three drivers to have been victorious in Formula 1, Indycars, NASCAR and top level sportscar racing.

He is both famous for constructing the Eagle cars which raced and won at Formula 1, Indycar and Sportscar level but also for being the first driver to spray the victor's champagne after winning the 1967 Le Mans 24 Hour race with A.J. Foyt for Ford. He is also known as the first Grand Prix driver to wear a full face crash helmet and for the Gurney flap, a mini-spoiler added to a rear wing to increase downforce.

The son of an opera singer, Dan moved with his family to California and at the age of 19 and became involved with the hot rod scene and started drag racing. After two years in the US Army he returned to racing, now in sportscars and his success caught the eye of Ferrari. He made his Formula 1 debut for them in 1959 but in the following years moved on to BRM and Porsche. His first victory was a surprising win for the Germans in the 1962 French GP. Further success followed with Brabham before he set up the Anglo American Racing Team to build the Weslake-powered cars in 1966. The following year he won the Belgian GP in the beautiful Eagle, a rare and the first ever win for an American car in Formula 1. He died in 2018. ARM

Not looking any older! Thirty years on, Dan with his magnificent Eagle Weslake at the Goodwood Festival of Speed.

Dan Gurney started the 1967 F1 season in fine style on 12 March at the Brands Hatch Race of Champions. The event was run over two 10 lap heats and a 40 lap final. Gurney won both heats with team mate Richie Ginther backing him up with third and second places.

In the final Gurney led from start to finish, despite pressure from Lorenzo Bandini's Ferrari.

Unfortunately the under-financed Eagle Weslake never quite achieved what it should have done. However, it remains one of the best looking F1 cars of all time. MT.

5
9
Martin Tomlinson

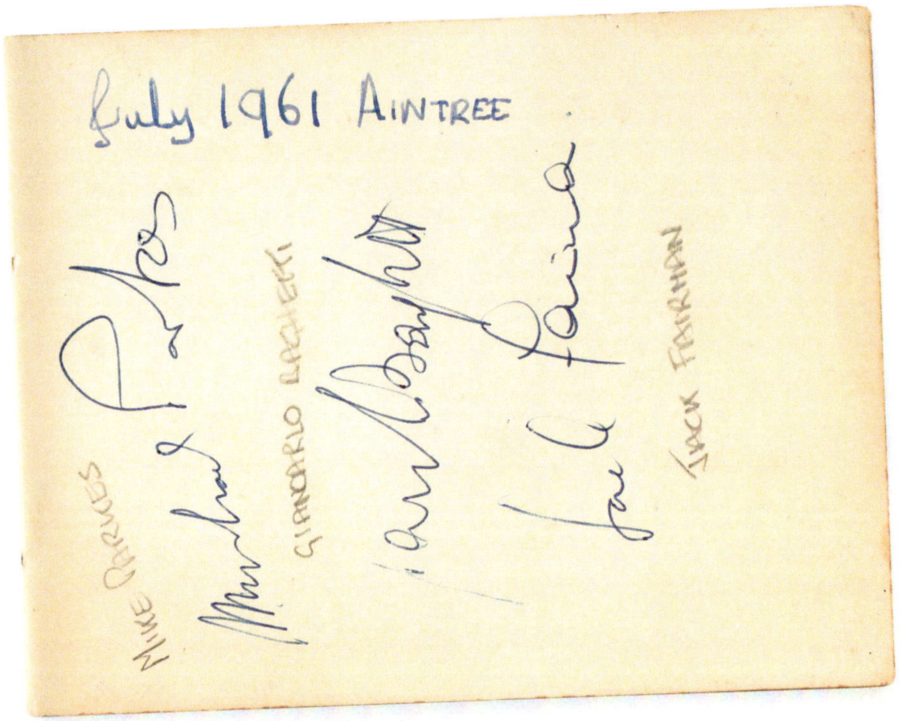

Mike Parkes

Mike Parkes was born into a motoring family – his father was the Chairman of Alvis Cars. But he made his name in Italy both as a driver and as a development engineer highly respected by Enzo Ferrari. He only competed in seven GPs in 1966 and 1967 and in the later year won the non-championship races at Silverstone and Syracuse. He had made his mark in sportscar racing and he scored many a success with various Ferraris including racing the Maranello Concessionaires 250GTO in the UK. He also won some of the biggest sportscar races including the Sebring 12 Hours, Monza 1000 Kms and finished second at Le Mans in 1967. He was tragically killed in a road accident in 1977. ARM

Giancarlo Baghetti

Milanese driver Giancarlo Baghetti has a special place in motor racing history – he is the only driver to have won his first three Formula 1 races. Driving for Ferrari in 1961, he had graduated from Formula Junior racing with the help of the Italian Federation and landed a seat in a sharknose Ferrari. Two of those wins came in non-championship races at Syracuse and in the Naples GP. But between them came a stunning victory in the French GP at Reims as his more illustrious team mates faltered. But he never won again and later drove for lesser teams. ARM

Giancarlo Baghetti wins his first F1 race - Ferrari 156 'Sharknose', Syracuse GP, 1961

Jack Fairman

Fairman raced both before and after the War. He completed in a handful of Formula 1 races for private teams and even raced the Ferguson 4-w-d car for Rob Walker. But in sportscar racing he was one of Moss' preferred co-drivers and together they won the 1959 Nürburgring 1000 Kms and the Goodwood Tourist Trophy for Aston Martin. ARM

Mike Parkes, Ferrari 250 SWB, Goodwood TT, 1961

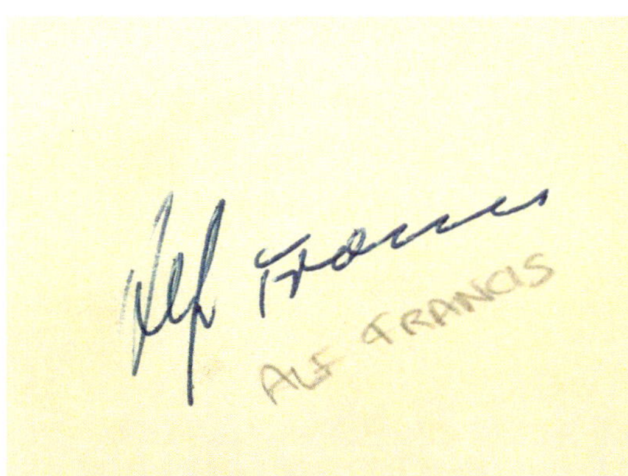

Alf Francis

Few mechanics became household names but one that did was Alf Francis - Stirling Moss' favoured spanner man and Chief Mechanic. Polish born Alfons Kowaleski changed his name when he arrived in Britain after WW2 and was taken under the wing of private team boss Rob Walker. As well as working on many of Stirling's cars he also helped develop the Walker Special. He subsequently moved to Italy and partnered gearbox expert Valerio Colotti. Later he emigrated to the US and died in 1983. His biography Alf Francis: Racing Mechanic makes fascinating reading. ARM

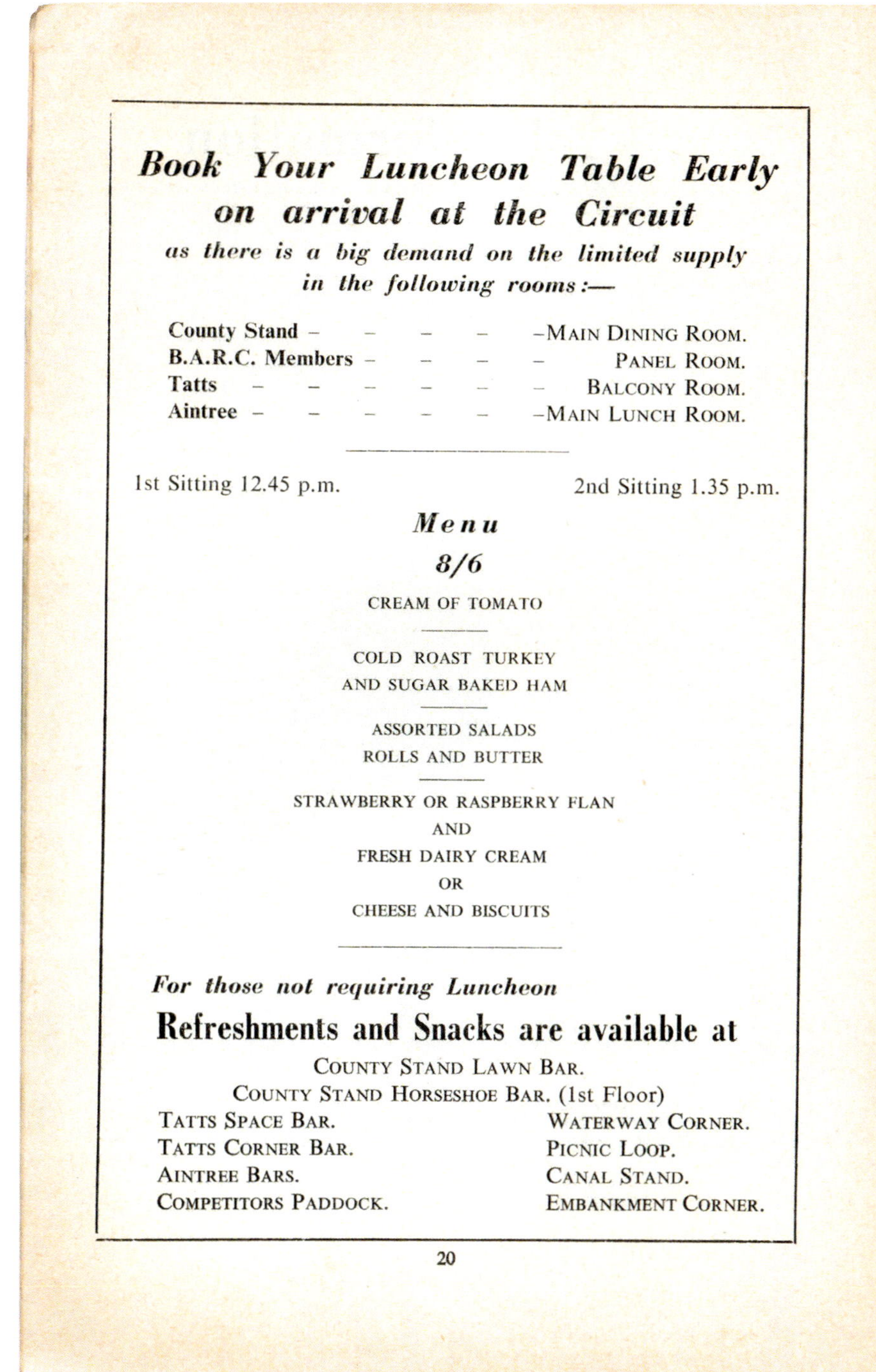

Book Your Luncheon Table Early on arrival at the Circuit

as there is a big demand on the limited supply in the following rooms:—

County Stand	Main Dining Room.
B.A.R.C. Members	Panel Room.
Tatts	Balcony Room.
Aintree	Main Lunch Room.

1st Sitting 12.45 p.m. 2nd Sitting 1.35 p.m.

Menu

8/6

CREAM OF TOMATO

COLD ROAST TURKEY
AND SUGAR BAKED HAM

ASSORTED SALADS
ROLLS AND BUTTER

STRAWBERRY OR RASPBERRY FLAN
AND
FRESH DAIRY CREAM
OR
CHEESE AND BISCUITS

For those not requiring Luncheon

Refreshments and Snacks are available at

County Stand Lawn Bar.
County Stand Horseshoe Bar. (1st Floor)

Tatts Space Bar.	Waterway Corner.
Tatts Corner Bar.	Picnic Loop.
Aintree Bars.	Canal Stand.
Competitors Paddock.	Embankment Corner.

20

We had cheese sandwiches instead. My Mum made them for us.

ADMISSION DETAILS OF TODAY'S

MOTOR CAR RACING AT AINTREE

Off course car parks open from 7 a.m.
On „ „ „ „ „ 8 a.m.
Stand and Turnstiles „ „ 9 a.m.

NOT BOOKABLE IN ADVANCE

	Children under 14 yrs. £ s. d.	Adults £ s. d.
STEEPLECHASE ENCLOSURE including the Big Embankment and the Picnic Loop	5 0	10 0
Limited unreserved accommodation in the Canal Stand will be available at an additional 2s. 6d.		
WEST ENCLOSURE	5 0	10 0
WATERWAY STAND—Limited unreserved accommodation will be available at an additional 7s. 6d		

BOOKABLE IN ADVANCE (or on the day, if available)

Advance booking at the reduced rates will close at 5 p.m. 3 days prior to a meeting.

	In Advance £ s. d.	On the Day £ s. d.
COUNTY STAND		
Reserved Balcony Seat (covered)	2 5 0	2 10 0
Reserved Roof seat (uncovered)	2 0 0	2 5 0
Recommended Car Parks—No. 1 Yellow or Central (situated within the Course).		
AINTREE AND TATTS STANDS		
Reserved Roof Seat (uncovered)	1 10 0	1 15 0
Recommended Car Park—Central (situated within the course).		
All Stand tickets include admission to the Promenade Enclosures.		
PROMENADE ENCLOSURES—Admission to the partly covered terraces in front of Aintree and/or Tatts Stands	1 2 6	1 5 0
Recommended Car Park—Central (situated within the course).		
All Stand and Promenade tickets include admission to the PADDOCK.		
COMBINED ADMISSION and on-the-course parking in the STEEPLECHASE or WEST ENCLOSURES.		
Car and two occupants	1 8 0	1 10 0
Car and all occupants	2 6 0	2 10 0
Motor-cycle combination and all passengers	1 17 0	2 0 0
Solo motor-cycle, driver and one passenger	1 3 0	1 5 0
N.B. Patrons visiting the STEEPLECHASE ENCLOSURE may park their cars in the Picnic Loop.		
Coaches (WEST ENCLOSURE only) :		
Single-deck and all occupants	14 10 0	16 0 0
Double-deck and all occupants	23 10 0	26 0 0

NO EXTRA CHARGE IS MADE FOR COMPETITOR'S PADDOCK TO AINTREE, TATTS, PROMENADE OR COUNTY STAND PATRONS.

CAR PARKS

Car Park locations are shown on the plan on pages 36-37.
It is advisable to book in advance.

The CENTRAL CAR PARK is situated within the course—vehicles will not be able to enter or leave except between races.

LAWN PADDOCK—County Stand patrons only	1 0 0	1 0 0
No. 1 Yellow—County Stand patrons only	10 0	10 0
Central—Stand and Promenade patrons only	10 0	10 0
Pass-out checks will NOT be available for the following car parks :		
No. 3 Red	10 0	10 0
Nos. 4 and 5 Red : 6 and 7 Green :	5 0	5 0
Motor-cycles : Combinations at car rate ; Solos at half car rate.		
COACHES		
Ormskirk Road Coach Park	1 0 0	1 0 0

Apply to:
AINTREE AUTOMOBILE RACING CO. LTD.
AINTREE, LIVERPOOL 9
Telephone: 3500 and 3550 Aintree

53

A Profit of Three Pounds, Five Bob!

There's an old saying 'The only way to make a small fortune out of motor racing is to start with a large one!' Motor sport is and always has been a money pit. So, on the rare occasion when you leave a race meeting financially in pocket it's an extremely memorable event.

One such occasion was the 1962 British GP at Aintree. We travelled in Maurice's Morris Oxford Farina across the Pennines to Aintree, on the outskirts of Liverpool. When we got there the traffic queuing to get into the circuit was at a standstill and the Grand Prix was due to start soon.

The traffic was so bad that the white-coated admission staff and local Constabulary were concerned. At this rate the race would start before all the spectators could get into the circuit and that would cause chaos. So in order to speed up the admission process the only alternative was to wave everyone through without stopping them in order to pay. So we got into the Tatts stand and the paddock for free! We were £3/5s (three pounds, five shillings) in profit at the end of the day! MT

Tri-ang present SCALEXTRIC

The world's most comprehensive electric model motor racing system!

Scalextric is the model motor racing system that comes closest to the real thing! There are a host of exclusive features; automatic lap counting, working public address system, cars with lights and track lighting for night racing, and—latest addition to the range—authentic vintage car models and motor cycle/side car combinations.

Call at your nearest toyshop or Sports dealer today for your copy of the Scalextric catalogue (price 9d.). See what a wonderfully realistic and exciting model system this is!

12

Every school boys' must have in 1962 was advertised in the race programme.

Jim Clark, Lotus 25, winner of the British GP, 1962

OULTON PARK

Oulton Park still retains its charm and atmosphere as one of Britain's old style circuits.

In the 1950's Maurice and his mates regularly officiated there as marshals. If I couldn't go, he would tell me about the day's racing, the drivers he had spoken to and the cars that he had seen. But one anecdote in particular has stayed with me; Stirling Moss had said to my Dad that "if Scott Brown gets into Old Hall Corner before me, I'll have a real problem in getting past him" Praise indeed for Archie.

The first time I visited the Cheshire circuit was in September 1961 for the Gold Cup. That day was the last time a front-engined car won a Formula1 race, when Stirling Moss beat strong opposition in a four-wheel-drive Ferguson Climax. Coincidentally my co-conspirator on this book was also there at his first Formula 1 race! MT

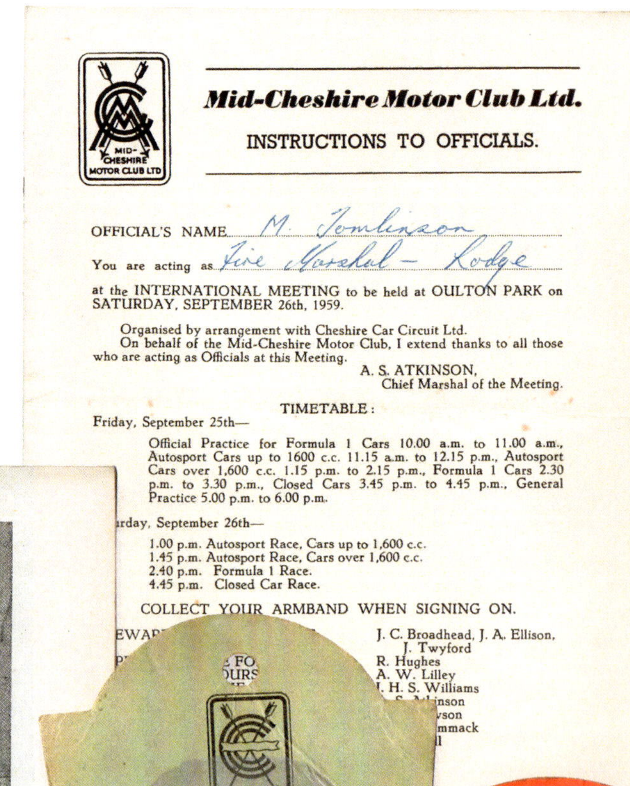

Mid-Cheshire Motor Club Ltd.

INSTRUCTIONS TO OFFICIALS.

OFFICIAL'S NAME M. Tomlinson

You are acting as Fire Marshal – Lodge

at the INTERNATIONAL MEETING to be held at OULTON PARK on SATURDAY, SEPTEMBER 26th, 1959.

Organised by arrangement with Cheshire Car Circuit Ltd.

On behalf of the Mid-Cheshire Motor Club, I extend thanks to all those who are acting as Officials at this Meeting.

A. S. ATKINSON,
Chief Marshal of the Meeting.

TIMETABLE:

Friday, September 25th—

Official Practice for Formula 1 Cars 10.00 a.m. to 11.00 a.m., Autosport Cars up to 1600 c.c. 11.15 a.m. to 12.15 p.m., Autosport Cars over 1,600 c.c. 1.15 p.m. to 2.15 p.m., Formula 1 Cars 2.30 p.m. to 3.30 p.m., Closed Cars 3.45 p.m. to 4.45 p.m., General Practice 5.00 p.m. to 6.00 p.m.

...rday, September 26th—

1.00 p.m. Autosport Race, Cars up to 1,600 c.c.
1.45 p.m. Autosport Race, Cars over 1,600 c.c.
2.40 p.m. Formula 1 Race.
4.45 p.m. Closed Car Race.

COLLECT YOUR ARMBAND WHEN SIGNING ON.

J. C. Broadhead, J. A. Ellison, J. Twyford
R. Hughes
A. W. Lilley

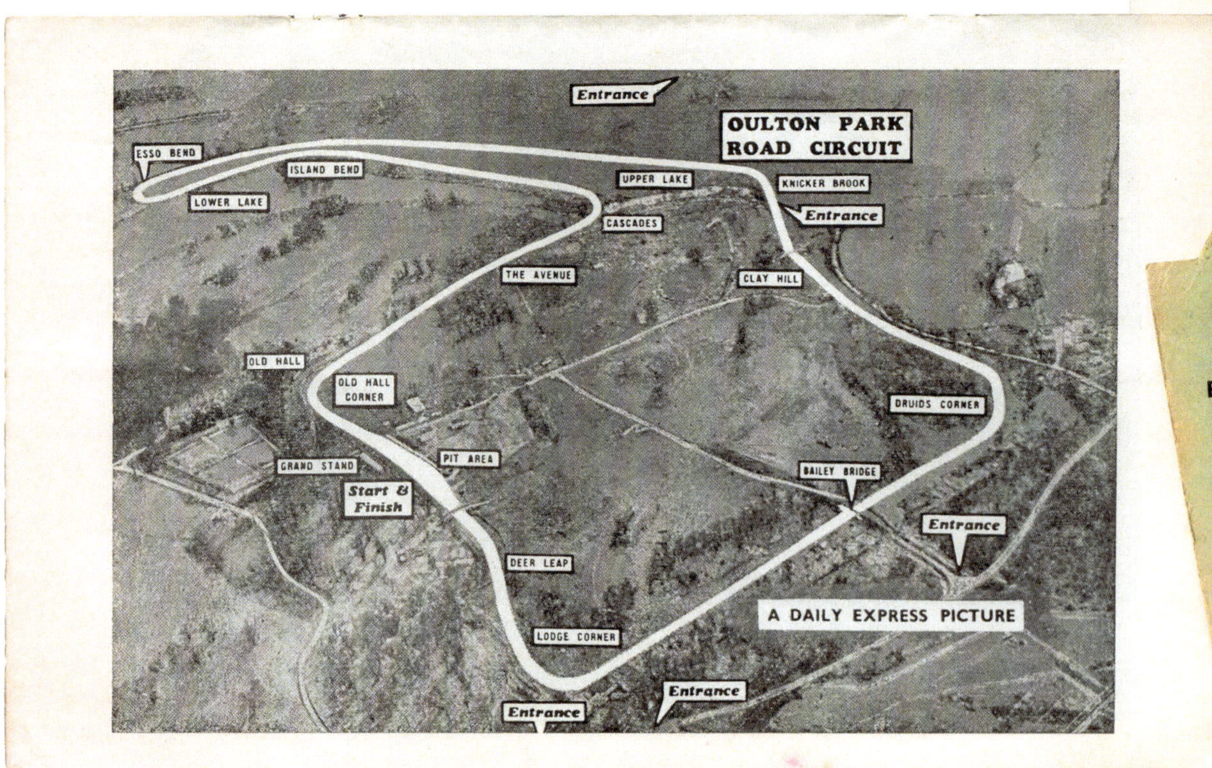

INTERNATIONAL GOLD CUP RACE

FOR FORMULA I RACING CARS

60 LAPS—165 MILES

No.	Driver	Entrant	Car
1	To be nominated	R. R. C. Walker Racing Team	Lotus-Coventry Climax
2	Jack Brabham	Cooper Car Co. Ltd.	Cooper-Coventry Climax
3	Bruce McLaren	Cooper Car Co. Ltd.	Cooper-Coventry Climax
4	Innes Ireland	Team Lotus	Lotus-Climax
5	Jim Clark	Team Lotus	Lotus-Climax
6	Trevor Taylor	Team Lotus	Lotus-Climax
7	Stirling Moss or Jack Fairman	R. R. C. Walker Racing Team	Ferguson-Coventry Climax
8	Graham Hill	Owen Racing Organisation	B.R.M. Coventry Climax
9	Tony Brooks	Owen Racing Organisation	B.R.M. Coventry Climax
10	Joakim Bonnier	Dr. ING.h.c.F.Porsche, K.G.	Porsche
11	Dan Gurney	Dr. ING.h.c.F.Porsche, K.G.	Porsche
12	Bernard Collomb	Driver	Cooper-Climax
14	Masten Gregory	U. D. T. Laystall Racing Team	Lotus-Climax
15	Henry Taylor	U. D. T. Laystall Racing Team	Lotus-Climax
16	Roy Salvadori	Yeoman Credit Racing Team	Yeoman Cooper-Coventry Climax
17	John Surtees	Yeoman Credit Racing Team	Yeoman Cooper-Coventry Climax
18	Tim Parnell	R. H. Parnell	Lotus-Climax
19	Brian Naylor	J. B. W. Car Co.	J. B. W. Climax
20	Chris Summers	Ansty Garage	Cooper-Climax
21	Jack Lewis	H. & L. Motors Ltd.	Cooper-Climax
22	Tony Marsh	Driver	B.R.M. Coventry Climax
23	Roger Revol	Driver	B.R.M. Coventry Climax
24	John Campbell-Jones	Driver	Cooper-Climax
25	David Piper	Gilby Engineering Co. Ltd.	Gilby-Coventry Climax
26	Graham Eden	G. R. Eden	Cooper-Climax
27	Gerald Ashmore	Driver	Lotus-Climax or Cooper-Climax
28	Wolfgang Seidel	Scuderia Colonia	Lotus-Coventry Climax
29	Michael May	Scuderia Colonia	Lotus-Coventry Climax
30	Ian Burgess (Reserve)	Ian Burgess	Cooper-Coventry Climax

21

International Gold Cup Race

FOR FORMULA I RACING CARS

73 LAPS—201 MILES **2-45 p.m.**

No.	Driver	Entrant	Car	Engine
1	**JACK BRABHAM** (Australia)	Brabham Racing Organisation Ltd.	Brabham	Coventry-Climax (8)
2	**BRUCE McLAREN** (New Zealand)	Cooper Car Co. Ltd.	Cooper	Coventry-Climax (8)
3	**JOHN SURTEES** (G.B.)	Lola Cars/Bowmaker	Lola	Coventry-Climax (8)
4	**ROY SALVADORI** (G.B.)	Lola Cars/Bowmaker	Lola	Coventry-Climax (8)
5	**GERALD ASHMORE** (G.B.)	Driver	Lotus	Coventry-Climax (4)
6	**GRAHAM EDEN** (G.B.)	Gerald Ashmore	Lotus	Coventry-Climax (4)
7	**CHRIS ASHMORE** (G.B.)	Driver	Lotus	Coventry-Climax (4)
8	**JIM CLARK** (G.B.)	Team Lotus	Lotus	Coventry-Climax (8)
9	**TREVOR TAYLOR** (G.B.)	Team Lotus	Lotus	Coventry-Climax (8)
10	**JACK LEWIS** (G.B.)	Ecurie Galloise	Cooper	Coventry-Climax (4)
11	**WOLFGANG SEIDEL** (Germany)	M. Seidel	Lotus	B.R.M. (8)
12	**GUNTER SEIFERT** (Germany)		Lotus	Coventry-Climax (4)
14	**INNES IRELAND** (G.B.)	U.D.T.-Laystall Racing Team	Lotus	Coventry-Climax (8) or B.R.M. (8)
15	**MASTEN GREGORY** (U.S.A.)	U.D.T.-Laystall Racing Team	Lotus	Coventry-Climax (8) or B.R.M. (8)
16	**PHILIP ROBINSON** (G.B.)	Driver	Lotus	Coventry-Climax (4)
17	**GRAHAM HILL** (G.B.)	Owen Racing Organisation	B.R.M.	B.R.M. (8)
18	**RICHIE GINTHER** (U.S.A.)	Owen Racing Organisation	B.R.M.	B.R.M. (8)
19	**BRUCE JOHNSTONE** (South Africa)	Owen Racing Organisation	B.R.M.	B.R.M. (8)
20	**KEITH GREENE** (G.B.)	Gilby Engineering Co. Ltd.	Gilby	B.R.M. (8)
21	**BERNARD COLLOMB** (France)	Driver	Cooper	Coventry-Climax (4)
22	**ANTHONY SHELLY** (U.S.A.)	John Dalton	Lotus	Coventry-Climax (4)
23	**GARY S. HOCKING** (South Africa)	R. H. H. Parnell	Lotus	Coventry-Climax (4)
24	**IAN BURGESS** (G.B.)	Anglo-American Equipe	Cooper	Coventry-Climax (4)
25	**C. G. de BEAUFORT** (Holland)	Ecurie Maasbergen	Porsche	Porsche (4)
26	**JOAKIM BONNIER** (Sweden)	R. R. C. Walker Racing Team	Lotus	Coventry-Climax (8)
27	**TONY SETTEMBER** (U.S.A.)	Emeryson Cars Ltd.	Emeryson	Coventry-Climax (4)

27

"I usually charge for this Old Boy."

Seven months after winning the Gold Cup, Stirling Moss had his career-ending crash at Goodwood. The nation held its breath. Slowly but surely he recovered from his injuries.

Meanwhile an eleven-year old enthusiast in Leeds wrote a poem wishing Moss a speedy recovery. On 1st September 1962, I took my poem with me to Oulton Park for the Gold Cup meeting, hoping to be able to give it to my hero.

I got my chance when Stirling Moss walked along the circuit grass verge towards Old Hall Corner where we were standing. I asked a nearby flag marshal if he could give the poem to "Mr Moss", which he duly did. Imagine how I felt when, after receiving the poem, Moss turned and waved in my direction! In the paddock later that day, I told Denis Jenkinson about the poem and asked if he wouldn't mind passing on my address to "Mr Moss". A few weeks later I received a signed letter from Stirling thanking me for "your charming poem". Unfortunately I have subsequently misplaced it

Thirty years later Stirling Moss was signing some prints of mine at his Mayfair home. Whilst he was doing so I mentioned to him that my Dad had marshalled at Oulton Park all those years ago. As it was his birthday in a few days time it would be nice if Stirling could sign his birthday card (which I just happened to have with me!). Unsurprisingly the response was "I usually charge for this Old Boy". But he didn't and here it is. MT

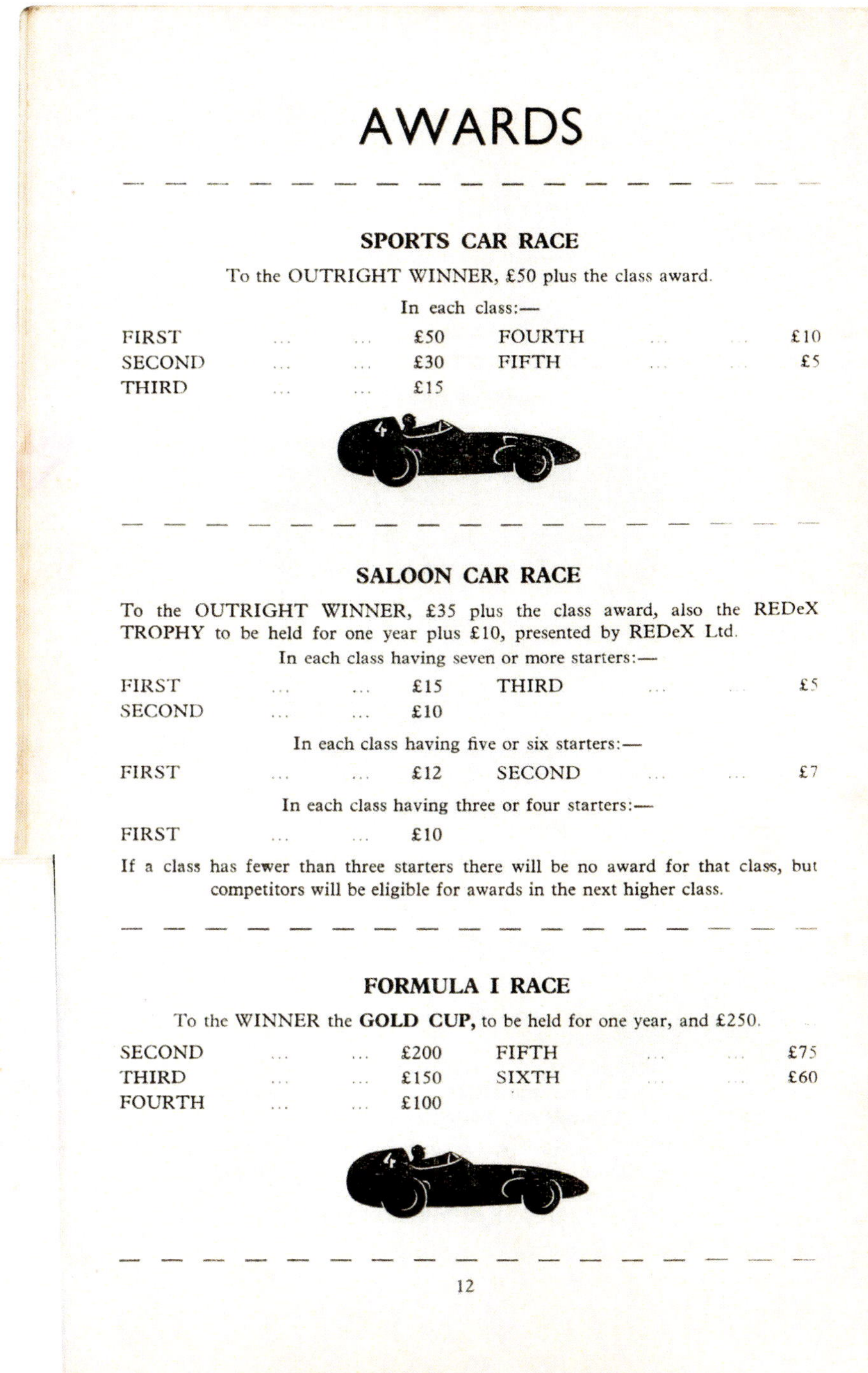

AWARDS

SPORTS CAR RACE

To the OUTRIGHT WINNER, £50 plus the class award.

In each class:—

FIRST	£50	FOURTH	£10
SECOND	£30	FIFTH	£5
THIRD	£15		

SALOON CAR RACE

To the OUTRIGHT WINNER, £35 plus the class award, also the REDeX TROPHY to be held for one year plus £10, presented by REDeX Ltd.

In each class having seven or more starters:—

FIRST	£15	THIRD	£5
SECOND	£10		

In each class having five or six starters:—

FIRST	£12	SECOND	£7

In each class having three or four starters:—

FIRST	£10

If a class has fewer than three starters there will be no award for that class, but competitors will be eligible for awards in the next higher class.

FORMULA I RACE

To the WINNER the **GOLD CUP,** to be held for one year, and £250.

SECOND	£200	FIFTH	£75
THIRD	£150	SIXTH	£60
FOURTH	£100		

12

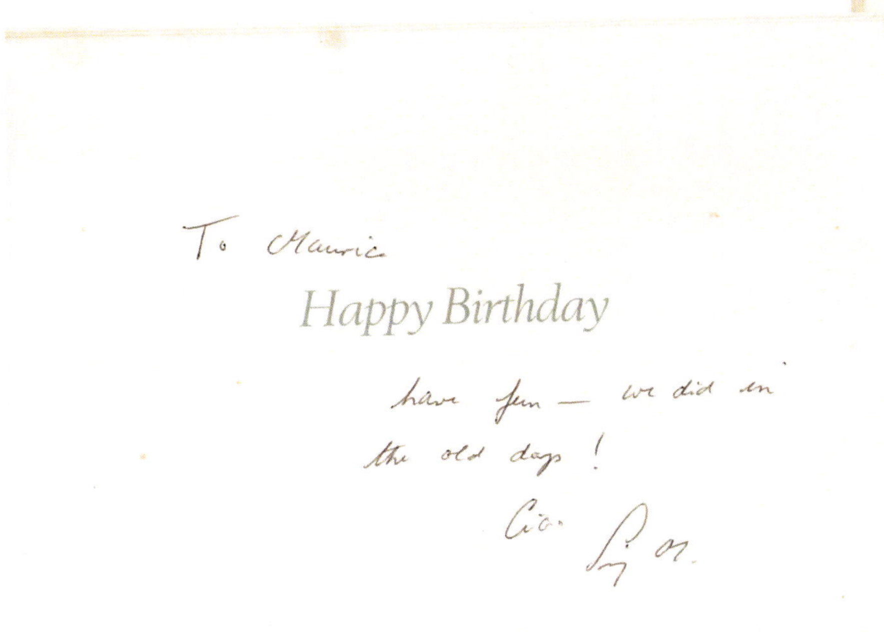

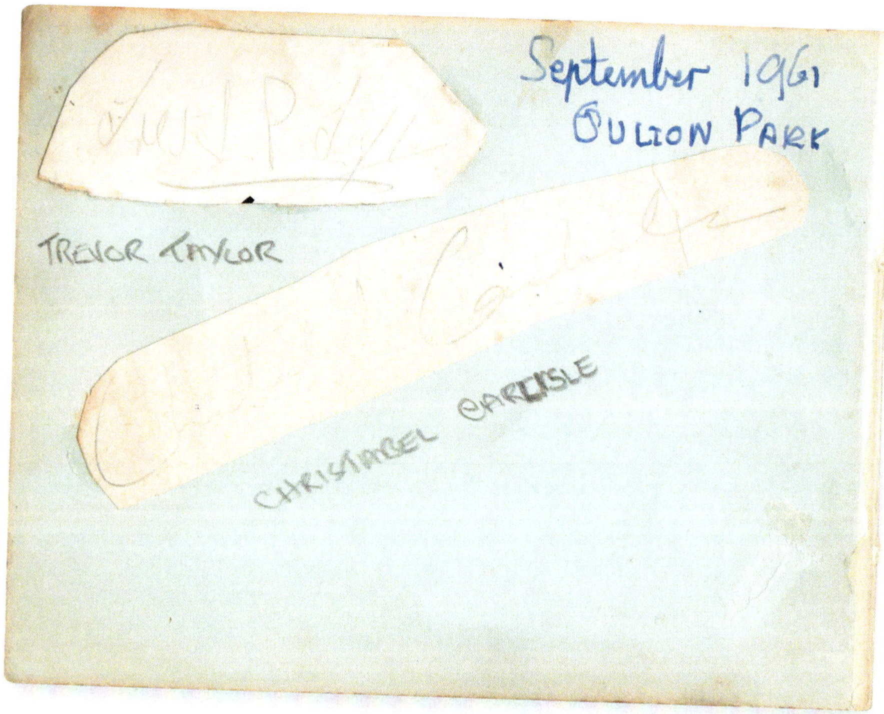

Trevor Taylor

When everyone else raced in blue overalls, the Yorkshireman Trevor Taylor raced in yellow complete with a yellow crash helmet. After a start in a 500cc F3 Cooper, he established himself as a rising star in 1958 by dominating the F3 Championship. Two years later he joined Team Lotus winning the Formula Junior category which earned him promotion to the Formula 1 team alongside Jim Clark. Apart from second place in the 1962 Dutch GP he was plagued with unreliability.

Colin Chapman let him go after three seasons and he joined the BRP team But he was an excellent all-rounder winning races in cars as diverse as a Lotus Elite and a Lola T70. His sister Anita was a good saloon car racer. He died aged 73. ARM

Christabel Carlisle

Christabel Carlisle was the first woman to make her mark, racing in touring cars in the British Saloon Car Championship. Her speed at the wheel of a Mini quickly caught the attention and in her second season, 1963 she scored a famous win at Goodwood with the Don Moore Mini. But she was also involved in several nasty accidents and retired from the sport. In 1965 she married a Baronet, Sir James Watson and became Lady Watson. She is a spritely 83-year old. ARM

Trevor Taylor, Lotus 24, second place Dutch GP, 1962

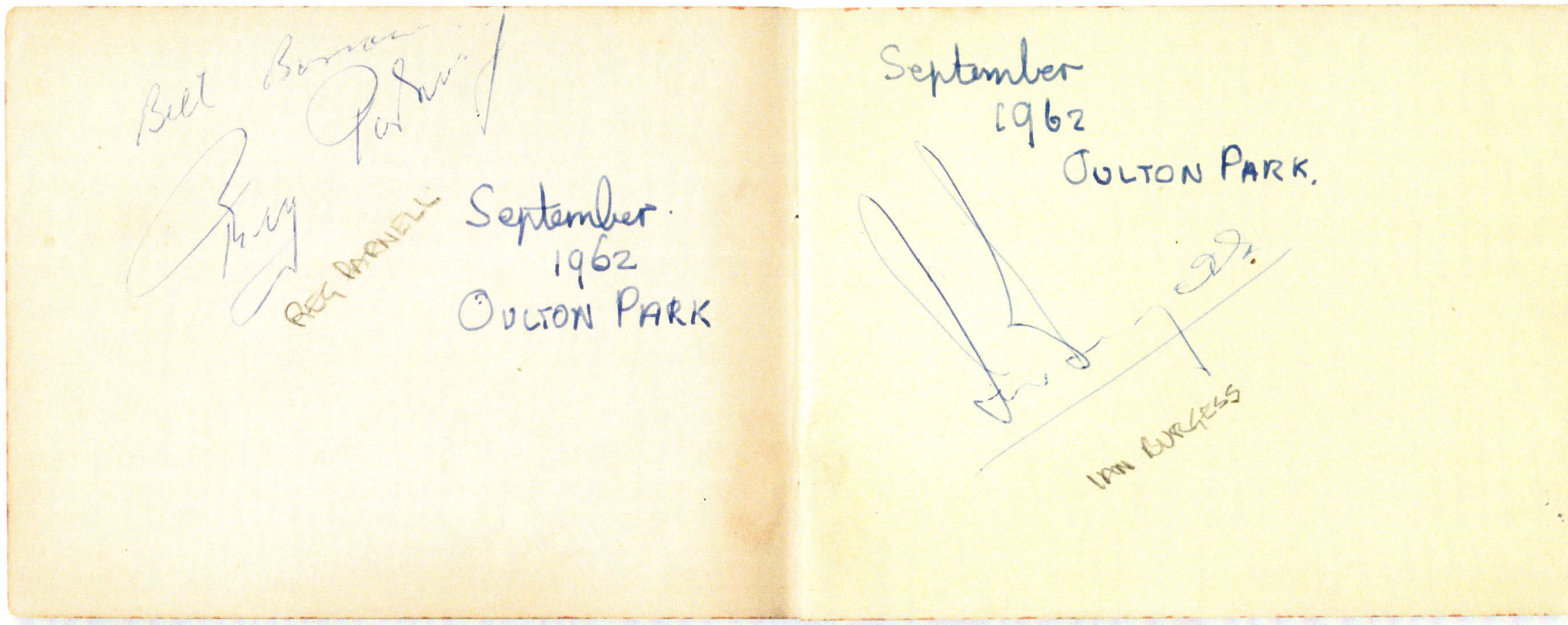

Reg Parnell

The Derby pig farmer Reg Parnell was one of the first Britain's to compete in the then new World Championship. Indeed he drove in the 1950 British GP at Silverstone in a factory Alfa Romeo. His earlier successes particularly at Goodwood emphasised his talent and professionalism. He had raced before WW2 and, in fact, the hostilities probably robbed Reg of his best racing years.

He later raced the Thinwall Special for Tony Vandervell and the problematical BRM V16. With a Ferrari T500 he had considerable success in non-championship races. On retirement he joined Aston Martin as their Team Manager and after ran his own privateer Formula 1 team. His son Tim followed in his footsteps both as a driver and team manager. ARM

Ian Burgess

Burgess' extensive career saw the Londoner taste early success in 500 cc Formula 3 cars and Formula 2. He was then a Formula 1 regular for privateers such as Scuderia Centro Sud and then American teams Camoradi International, Louise Bryden-Brown and Hugh Powell's Scirocco-BRMs. He started in some 20 GPs. In later life he was caught up in the drugs trade and spent ten years in prison for smuggling heroin. He died aged 81. ARM

Reg Parnell, 'Thinwall Special', winner BRDC International Trophy, Silverstone, 1951

SILVERSTONE

The first time I was taken to Silverstone was to watch the 101 lap British GP in 1956. A stellar entry of 29 included all the top drivers of the day. We stood at Maggotts where the crowd was packed in behind the paling fence making it difficult to see very much. However, being a small boy I was able to worm my way to the front assisted by a group of firemen who were stood in front of us. So in the end I got a good view of the race, which was not the case for Maurice and Charlie who were still standing several rows back.

In 1965 I witnessed one of Jim Clark's finest races at the British GP. Clark had built up a lead of half a lap over second place Graham Hill. But all was not well with his Lotus - the engine was misfiring and was losing oil causing the level in the tank to drop. To counter this Clark was having to coast round the corners and only using the power on the straights. The result was that the determined Hill was closing. In the end he didn't quite catch Clark, but it made for an exciting last few laps.

An added attraction at the British GP in 1967 was the a demonstration of historic cars by members of the 'Club International des Ancien Pilotes de Grand Prix.' I managed to get the signatures of some of these legends who are mentioned later in this chapter. MT

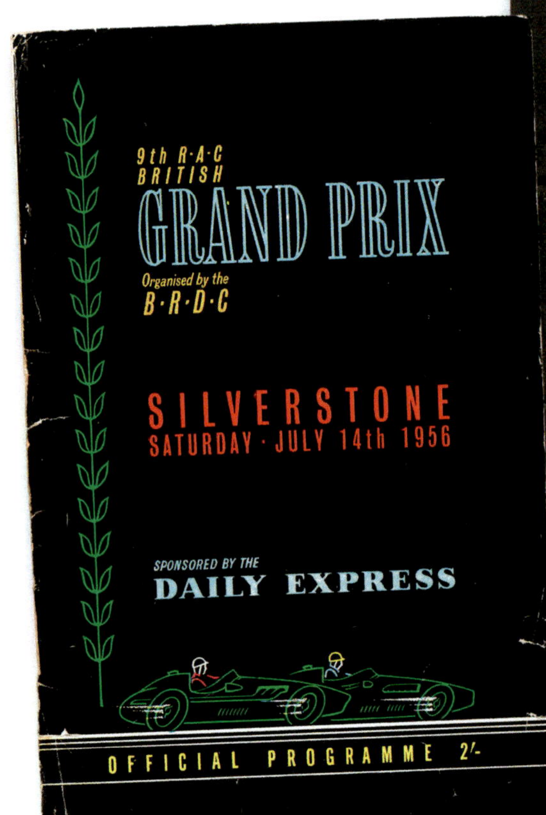

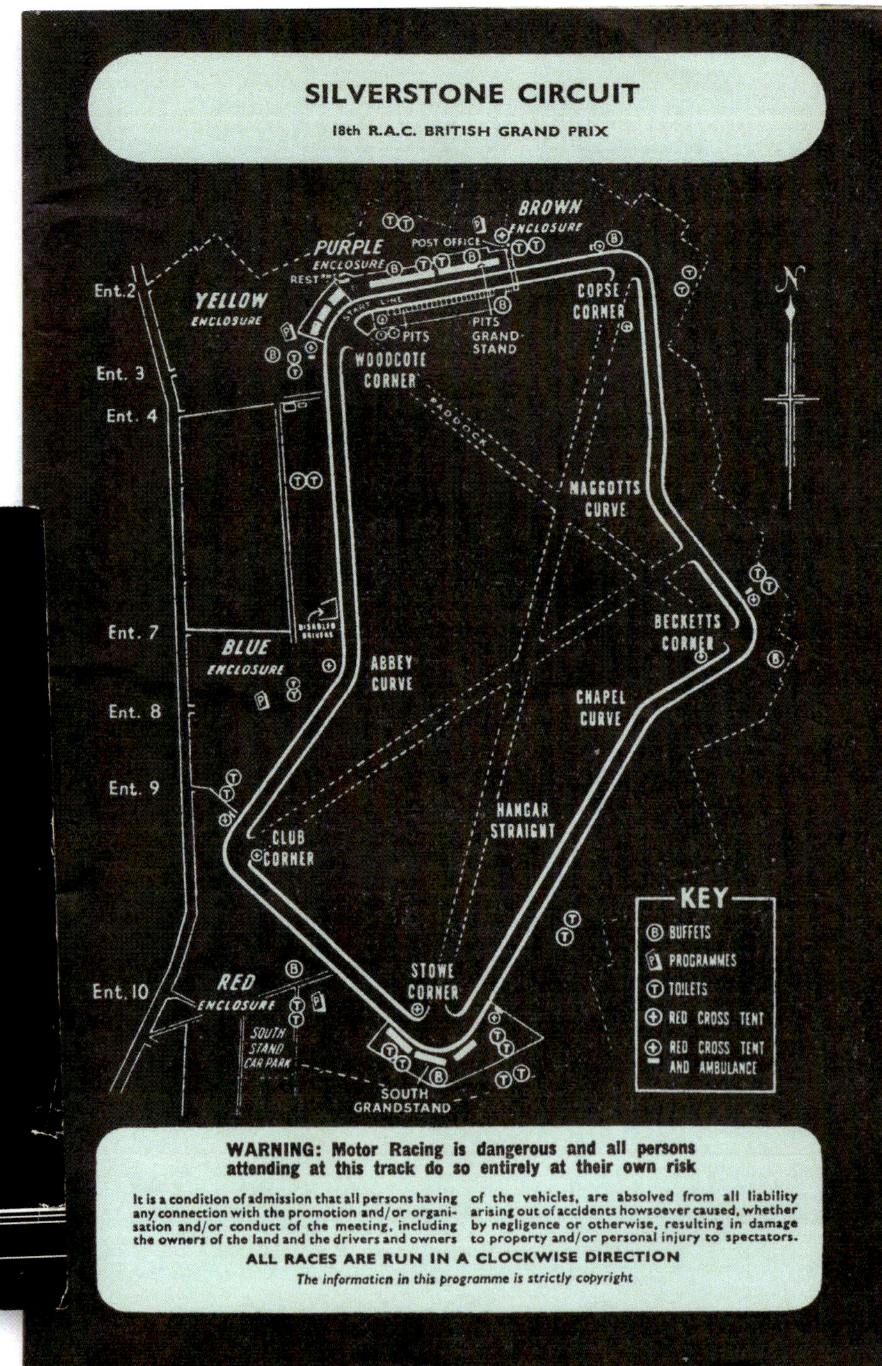

TROPHIES AND AWARDS

The 18th R.A.C. British Grand Prix

To the entrant of the car finishing:

1st The Mervyn O'Gorman Trophy (Perpetual) and £1000.
2nd £500. 3rd. £300. 4th £200. 5th £150. 6th £100.
Fastest practice lap on each practice day £100.

To the entrant of the first British Driver:

The Fred Cramer Trophy

International Sports Car Race

To the entrant of the car recording the highest average speed:

1st The Senior Service Trophy and £100.
2nd £70. 3rd £50.

IN EACH CLASS:

No. of starters	1st	2nd	3rd
9 or more	£100	£50	£25
6. 7. 8.	£80	£40	£20
4. 5.	£60	£30	£15
3.	£30	£15	—

International Touring Car Race

To the entrant of the car recording the highest average speed:

1st The Britax Trophy and £70.
Class awards as for Sports Car Race.

International Formula 3 Race

To the entrant of the car finishing:

1st A B.R.D.C. Trophy and £100.
2nd £50. 3rd £25. 4th £15.
All cash awards go to the entrant.

15

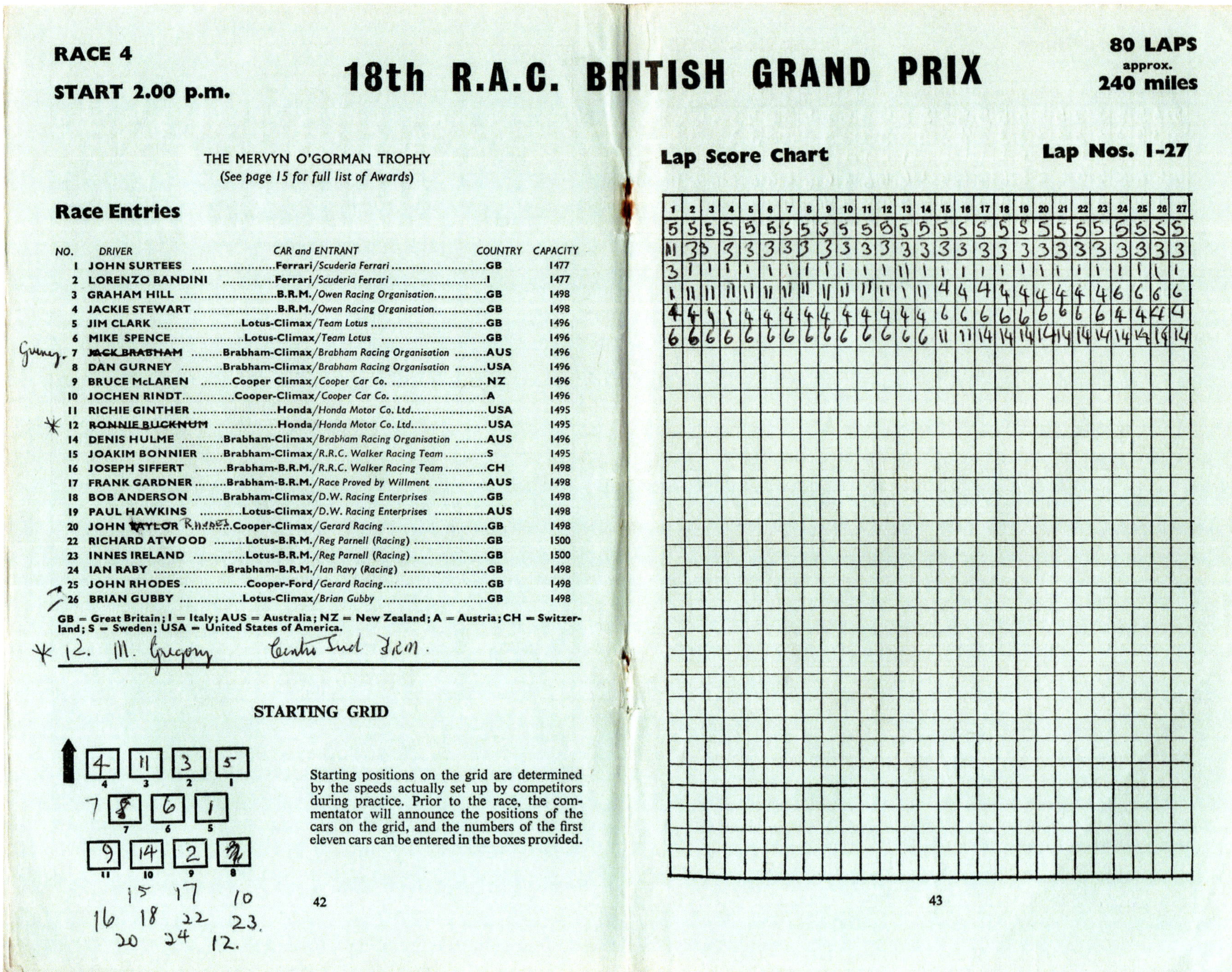

RACE 4

START 2.00 p.m.

18th R.A.C. BRITISH GRAND PRIX

80 LAPS
approx.
240 miles

THE MERVYN O'GORMAN TROPHY
(See page 15 for full list of Awards)

Race Entries

NO.	DRIVER	CAR and ENTRANT	COUNTRY	CAPACITY
1	JOHN SURTEES	Ferrari/*Scuderia Ferrari*	GB	1477
2	LORENZO BANDINI	Ferrari/*Scuderia Ferrari*	I	1477
3	GRAHAM HILL	B.R.M./*Owen Racing Organisation*	GB	1498
4	JACKIE STEWART	B.R.M./*Owen Racing Organisation*	GB	1498
5	JIM CLARK	Lotus-Climax/*Team Lotus*	GB	1496
6	MIKE SPENCE	Lotus-Climax/*Team Lotus*	GB	1496
Gurney. 7	~~JACK BRABHAM~~	Brabham-Climax/*Brabham Racing Organisation*	AUS	1496
8	DAN GURNEY	Brabham-Climax/*Brabham Racing Organisation*	USA	1496
9	BRUCE McLAREN	Cooper Climax/*Cooper Car Co.*	NZ	1496
10	JOCHEN RINDT	Cooper-Climax/*Cooper Car Co.*	A	1496
11	RICHIE GINTHER	Honda/*Honda Motor Co. Ltd.*	USA	1495
* 12	~~RONNIE BUCKNUM~~	Honda/*Honda Motor Co. Ltd.*	USA	1495
14	DENIS HULME	Brabham-Climax/*Brabham Racing Organisation*	AUS	1496
15	JOAKIM BONNIER	Brabham-Climax/*R.R.C. Walker Racing Team*	S	1495
16	JOSEPH SIFFERT	Brabham-B.R.M./*R.R.C. Walker Racing Team*	CH	1498
17	FRANK GARDNER	Brabham-B.R.M./*Race Proved by Willment*	AUS	1498
18	BOB ANDERSON	Brabham-Climax/*D.W. Racing Enterprises*	GB	1498
19	PAUL HAWKINS	Lotus-Climax/*D.W. Racing Enterprises*	AUS	1498
20	JOHN ~~TAYLOR~~ Rhodes	Cooper-Climax/*Gerard Racing*	GB	1498
22	RICHARD ATWOOD	Lotus-B.R.M./*Reg Parnell (Racing)*	GB	1500
23	INNES IRELAND	Lotus-B.R.M./*Reg Parnell (Racing)*	GB	1500
24	IAN RABY	Brabham-B.R.M./*Ian Ravy (Racing)*	GB	1498
25	JOHN RHODES	Cooper-Ford/*Gerard Racing*	GB	1498
26	BRIAN GUBBY	Lotus-Climax/*Brian Gubby*	GB	1498

GB = Great Britain; I = Italy; AUS = Australia; NZ = New Zealand; A = Austria; CH = Switzerland; S = Sweden; USA = United States of America.

* 12. M. Gregory Centro Sud BRM.

STARTING GRID

4	11	3	5
4	3	2	1
8	6	1	
7	6	5	
9	14	2	7
11	10	9	8

15 17 10
16 18 22 23.
20 24 12.

Starting positions on the grid are determined by the speeds actually set up by competitors during practice. Prior to the race, the commentator will announce the positions of the cars on the grid, and the numbers of the first eleven cars can be entered in the boxes provided.

42

Lap Score Chart

Lap Nos. 1-27

1	2	3	4	5	6	7	8	9	10	11	12	13	14	15	16	17	18	19	20	21	22	23	24	25	26	27
5	5	5	5	5	5	5	5	5	5	5	5	5	5	5	5	5	5	5	5	5	5	5	5	5	5	5
11	3	3	3	3	3	3	3	3	3	3	3	3	3	3	3	3	3	3	3	3	3	3	3	3	3	3
3	1	1	1	1	1	1	1	1	1	1	1	11	1	1	1	1	1	1	1	1	1	1	1	1	1	1
1	11	11	11	11	11	11	11	11	11	11	11	1	11	4	4	4	4	4	4	4	4	4	6	6	6	6
4	4	4	4	4	4	4	4	4	4	4	4	4	4	6	6	6	6	6	6	6	6	6	4	4	4	4
6	6	6	6	6	6	6	6	6	6	6	6	6	6	11	11	14	14	14	14	14	14	14	14	14	14	14

43

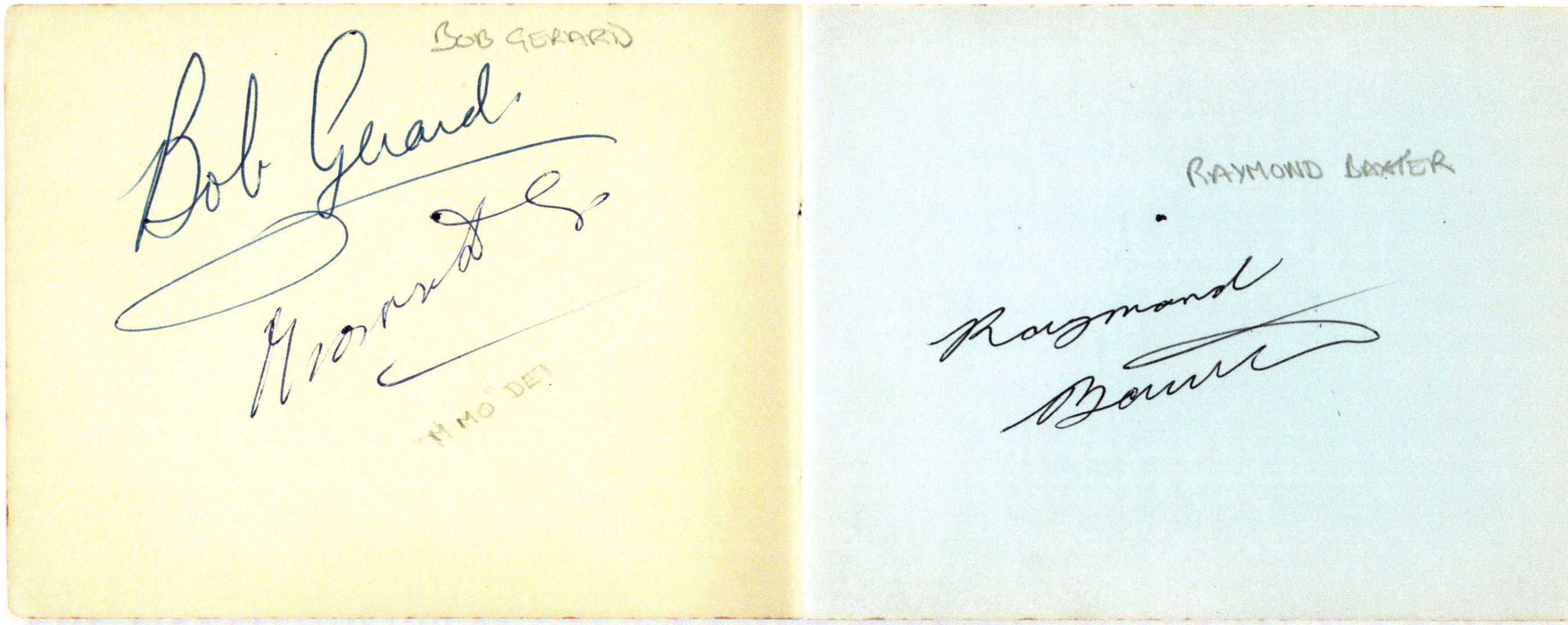

Bob Gerard, Cooper-Bristol, Crystal Palace, 30th July 1955

Bob Gerard

Like his near neighbour Reg Parnell, Bob Gerard's career straddled WW2. Success came with an ERA in which he won the British Empire Trophy race in 1947,1948 and 1949. In 1949 he came a close second in the British G.P. He later moved on to a Cooper Climax and in all had eight Grand Prix starts, mainly at Silverstone. "Mr Bob", as he was affectionately known, went on run a Formula 2 team, often giving an early chance to emerging talent. ARM

Mimo Dei

Italian 1950s privateer Formula 1 entrant Gugliemo "Mimo" Dei is perhaps the rarest and most obscure autograph in Martin's book. Dei was a Maserati dealer for Central and Southern Italy so called his team Scuderia Centro Sud. Masten Gregory and Lorenzo Bandini were amongst his drivers. ARM

Raymond Baxter

A former World War 11 fighter pilot, Raymond Baxter was BBC TV's first and highly knowledgeable Grand Prix commentator. A great broadcaster he went on to present other BBC programmes such as Tomorrow's World and provided radio commentary for the late Queen's coronation. ARM

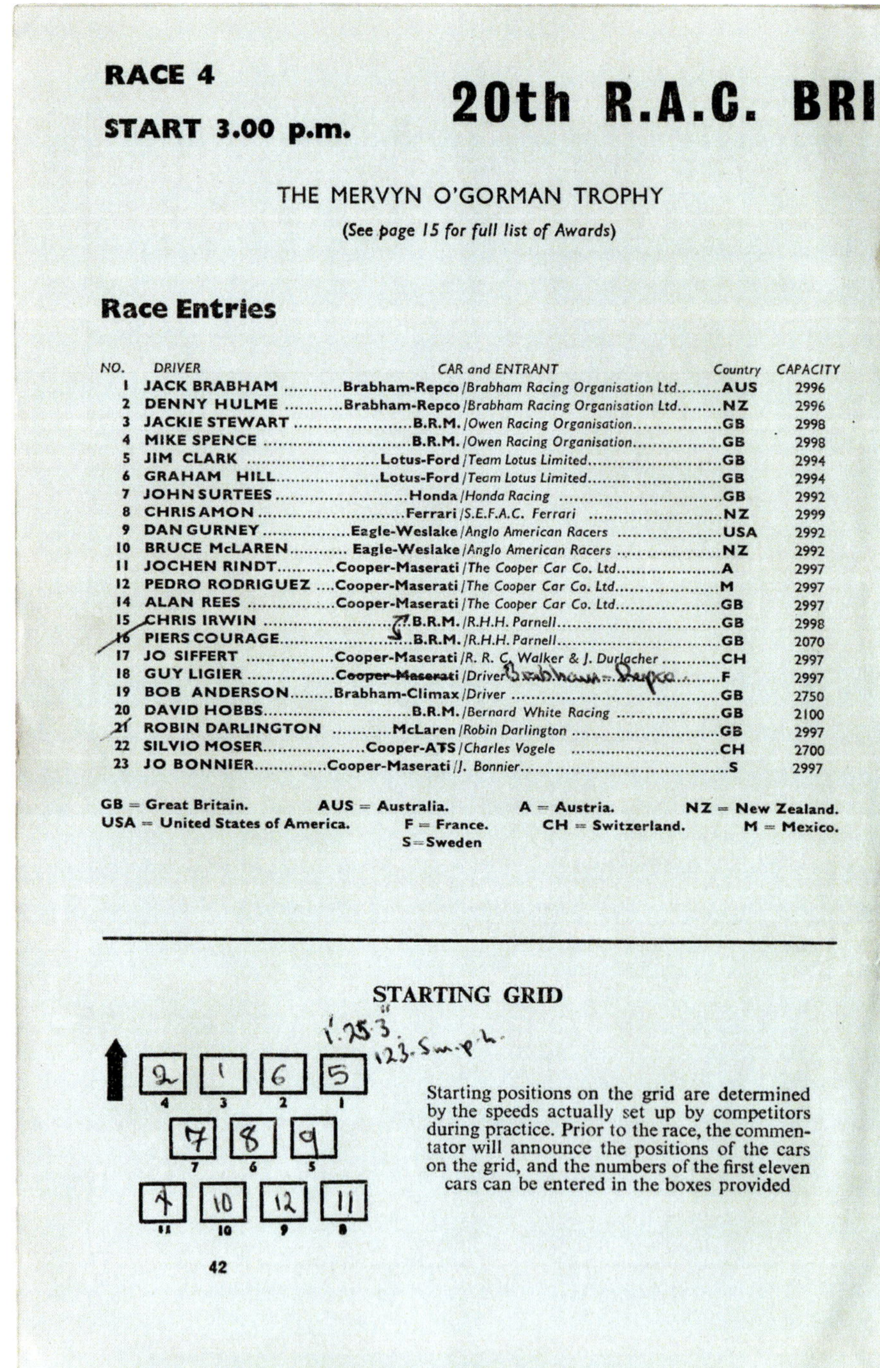

RACE 4

START 3.00 p.m.

20th R.A.C. BRIT

THE MERVYN O'GORMAN TROPHY

(See page 15 for full list of Awards)

Race Entries

NO.	DRIVER	CAR and ENTRANT	Country	CAPACITY
1	JACK BRABHAM	Brabham-Repco / *Brabham Racing Organisation Ltd*	AUS	2996
2	DENNY HULME	Brabham-Repco / *Brabham Racing Organisation Ltd*	NZ	2996
3	JACKIE STEWART	B.R.M. / *Owen Racing Organisation*	GB	2998
4	MIKE SPENCE	B.R.M. / *Owen Racing Organisation*	GB	2998
5	JIM CLARK	Lotus-Ford / *Team Lotus Limited*	GB	2994
6	GRAHAM HILL	Lotus-Ford / *Team Lotus Limited*	GB	2994
7	JOHN SURTEES	Honda / *Honda Racing*	GB	2992
8	CHRIS AMON	Ferrari / *S.E.F.A.C. Ferrari*	NZ	2999
9	DAN GURNEY	Eagle-Weslake / *Anglo American Racers*	USA	2992
10	BRUCE McLAREN	Eagle-Weslake / *Anglo American Racers*	NZ	2992
11	JOCHEN RINDT	Cooper-Maserati / *The Cooper Car Co. Ltd*	A	2997
12	PEDRO RODRIGUEZ	Cooper-Maserati / *The Cooper Car Co. Ltd*	M	2997
14	ALAN REES	Cooper-Maserati / *The Cooper Car Co. Ltd*	GB	2997
15	CHRIS IRWIN	B.R.M. / *R.H.H. Parnell*	GB	2998
16	PIERS COURAGE	B.R.M. / *R.H.H. Parnell*	GB	2070
17	JO SIFFERT	Cooper-Maserati / *R. R. C. Walker & J. Durlacher*	CH	2997
18	GUY LIGIER	Cooper-Maserati / *Driver*	F	2997
19	BOB ANDERSON	Brabham-Climax / *Driver*	GB	2750
20	DAVID HOBBS	B.R.M. / *Bernard White Racing*	GB	2100
21	ROBIN DARLINGTON	McLaren / *Robin Darlington*	GB	2997
22	SILVIO MOSER	Cooper-ATS / *Charles Vogele*	CH	2700
23	JO BONNIER	Cooper-Maserati / *J. Bonnier*	S	2997

GB = Great Britain. AUS = Australia. A = Austria. NZ = New Zealand.
USA = United States of America. F = France. CH = Switzerland. M = Mexico.
S = Sweden

STARTING GRID

4 3 2 1
7 6 5
11 10 9 8

Starting positions on the grid are determined by the speeds actually set up by competitors during practice. Prior to the race, the commentator will announce the positions of the cars on the grid, and the numbers of the first eleven cars can be entered in the boxes provided

42

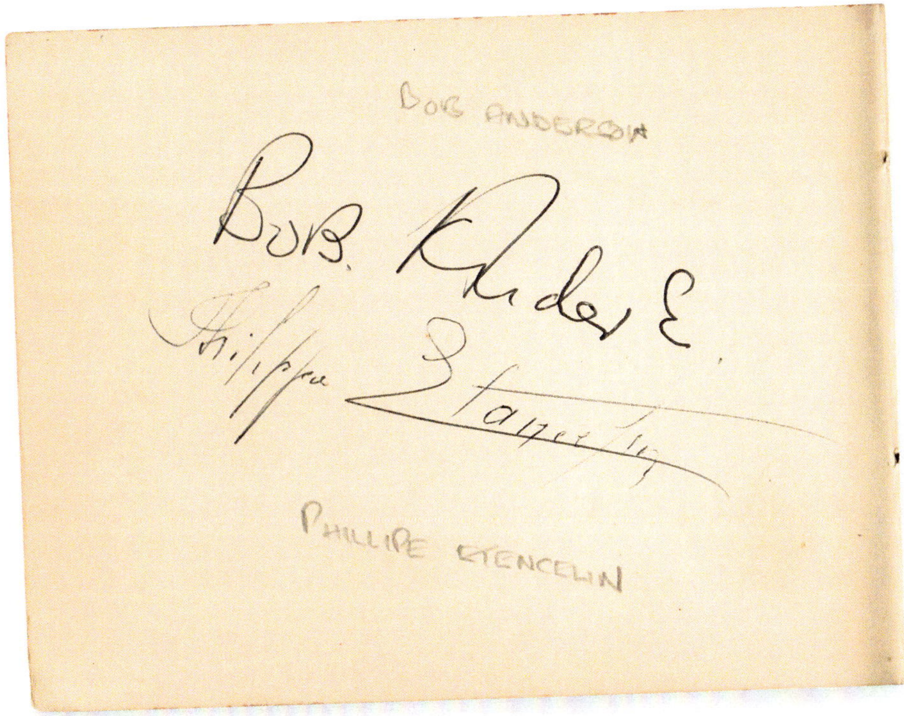

Bob Anderson's podium finish, Brabham Climax, Austrian GP, 1964

Philippe 'Phi Phi' Étancelin, Lago Talbot, Grand Prix d'Europe, 1951

Bob Anderson

Robert Hugh Fearon Anderson raced Grand Prix motorcycles from 1958 to 1960 winning the North West 200 road race twice. He then made the difficult switch to four wheels and after a year in Formula Junior became a privateer Formula 1 driver/entrant in 1963 and 1964, with a second-hand Lola and then a Brabham. He was killed testing the Brabham at Silverstone in 1967. ARM

Philippe Étancelin

Étancelin, known as "Phi Phi", is one of the rarest autographs in the collection. Born in Rouen in 1896 he didn't start racing until he was 30. Before the War he raced Bugattis Alfas, Maseratis and Talbots in the major races in Europe. He won the 1934 Le Mans 24 Hours in an Alfa Romeo 8C. He raced a Talbot-Lago in the first ever World Championship race and finished 8th. Throughout his career which lasted until the early 1950s, he raced in a flat cap worn backwards. ARM

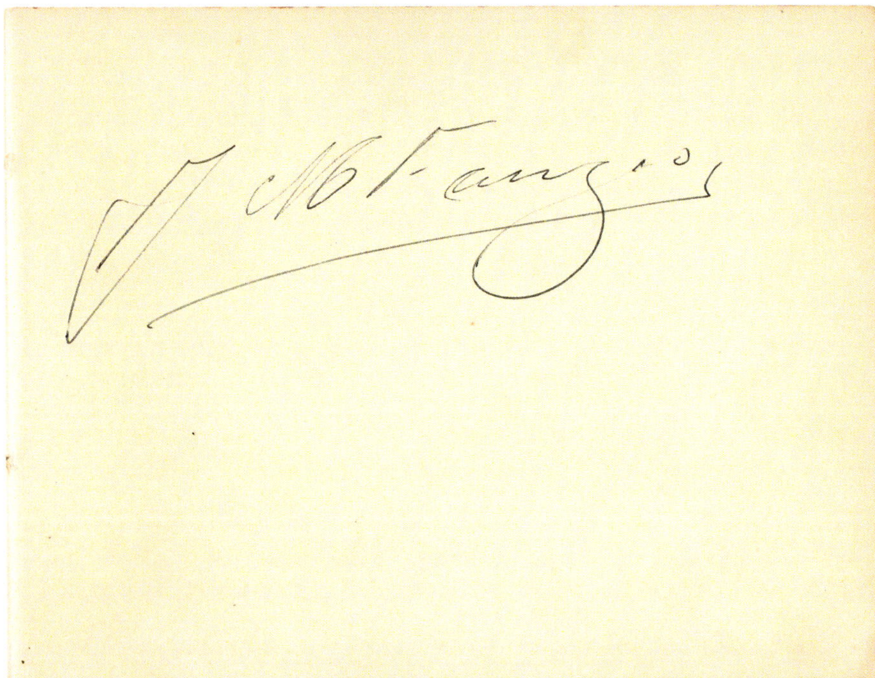

Juan Manuel Fangio

The Argentine racer was one of the greatest of all time and his rare signature is one of the most prominent in the whole collection. The man from Balcarce was something of a late starter but he went on to win the World Championship on no fewer than five occasions and was the dominant driver of the first decade of the series. Driving variously for Mercedes-Benz, Ferrari and Maserati, he took the first title in 1951 and then each year from 1954 to 1957.

His competition career started in 1936 in the Tourismo Carretera series in Argentina in a Ford V8 and won the title for several years and also dominated several long distance and highly dangerous road races. This success prompted the Argentine Automobile Club to buy him a Maserati and send him to Europe in 1949. By now he was in his early 30s and older than most of his rivals.

He was signed by Alfa Romeo for the 1950 season, but retired in the opening British GP. He then went on to win the Monaco GP in the 158 and won again in Belgium and France. He finished second in his "rookie" World Championship year and won it a year later. In 1952 he joined Maserati and was second in the Championship the following year. Then came a run of four consecutive titles in various different makes of car, his last at the age of 46. His winning percentage in the World Championship was almost 50% and included 24 victories. He retired in 1958, continued as a regular visitor to motor sports events and died aged 84 in 1995. ARM

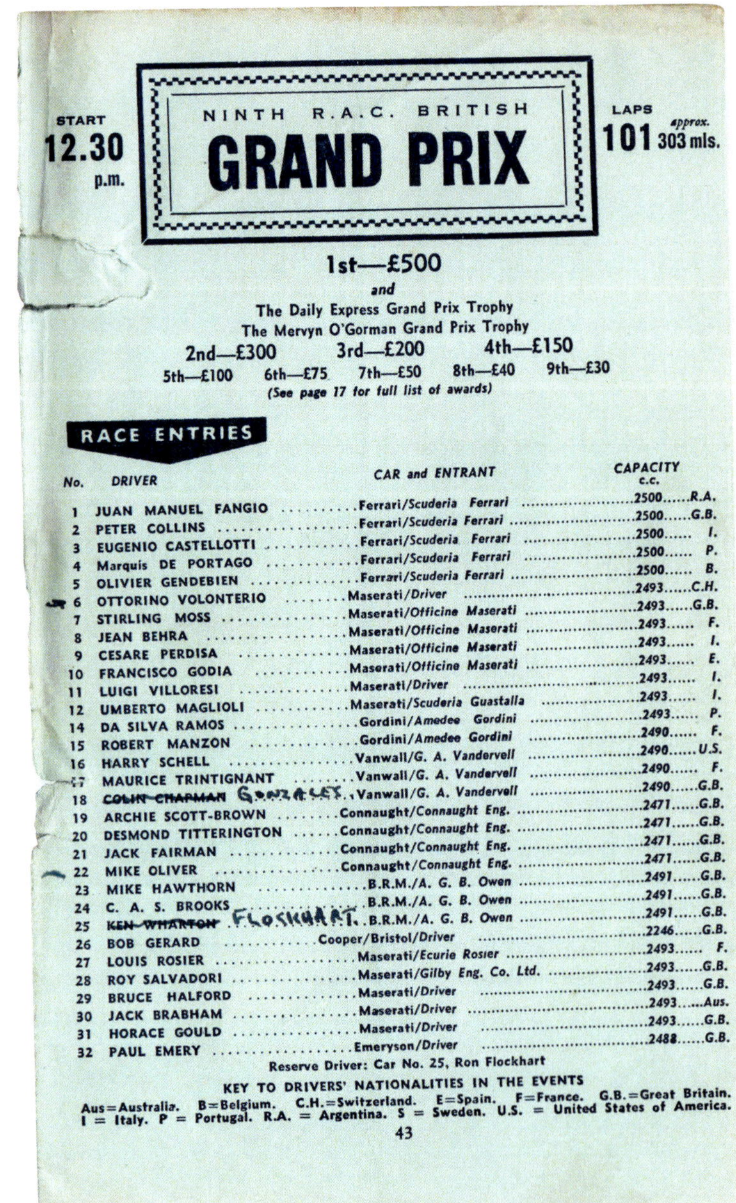

START 12.30 p.m.

NINTH R.A.C. BRITISH

GRAND PRIX

LAPS 101 approx. 303 mls.

1st—£500

and

The Daily Express Grand Prix Trophy

The Mervyn O'Gorman Grand Prix Trophy

2nd—£300 3rd—£200 4th—£150

5th—£100 6th—£75 7th—£50 8th—£40 9th—£30

(See page 17 for full list of awards)

RACE ENTRIES

No.	DRIVER	CAR and ENTRANT	CAPACITY c.c.	
1	JUAN MANUEL FANGIO	Ferrari/Scuderia Ferrari	2500	R.A.
2	PETER COLLINS	Ferrari/Scuderia Ferrari	2500	G.B.
3	EUGENIO CASTELLOTTI	Ferrari/Scuderia Ferrari	2500	I.
4	Marquis DE PORTAGO	Ferrari/Scuderia Ferrari	2500	P.
5	OLIVIER GENDEBIEN	Ferrari/Scuderia Ferrari	2500	B.
6	OTTORINO VOLONTERIO	Maserati/Driver	2493	C.H.
7	STIRLING MOSS	Maserati/Officine Maserati	2493	G.B.
8	JEAN BEHRA	Maserati/Officine Maserati	2493	F.
9	CESARE PERDISA	Maserati/Officine Maserati	2493	I.
10	FRANCISCO GODIA	Maserati/Officine Maserati	2493	E.
11	LUIGI VILLORESI	Maserati/Driver	2493	I.
12	UMBERTO MAGLIOLI	Maserati/Scuderia Guastalla	2493	I.
14	DA SILVA RAMOS	Gordini/Amedee Gordini	2493	P.
15	ROBERT MANZON	Gordini/Amedee Gordini	2490	F.
16	HARRY SCHELL	Vanwall/G. A. Vandervell	2490	U.S.
17	MAURICE TRINTIGNANT	Vanwall/G. A. Vandervell	2490	F.
18	~~COLIN CHAPMAN~~ GONZALEZ	Vanwall/G. A. Vandervell	2490	G.B.
19	ARCHIE SCOTT-BROWN	Connaught/Connaught Eng.	2471	G.B.
20	DESMOND TITTERINGTON	Connaught/Connaught Eng.	2471	G.B.
21	JACK FAIRMAN	Connaught/Connaught Eng.	2471	G.B.
22	MIKE OLIVER	Connaught/Connaught Eng.	2471	G.B.
23	MIKE HAWTHORN	B.R.M./A. G. B. Owen	2491	G.B.
24	C. A. S. BROOKS	B.R.M./A. G. B. Owen	2491	G.B.
25	~~KEN WHARTON~~ FLOCKHART.	B.R.M./A. G. B. Owen	2491	G.B.
26	BOB GERARD	Cooper/Bristol/Driver	2246	G.B.
27	LOUIS ROSIER	Maserati/Ecurie Rosier	2493	F.
28	ROY SALVADORI	Maserati/Gilby Eng. Co. Ltd.	2493	G.B.
29	BRUCE HALFORD	Maserati/Driver	2493	G.B.
30	JACK BRABHAM	Maserati/Driver	2493	Aus.
31	HORACE GOULD	Maserati/Driver	2493	G.B.
32	PAUL EMERY	Emeryson/Driver	2488	G.B.

Reserve Driver: Car No. 25, Ron Flockhart

KEY TO DRIVERS' NATIONALITIES IN THE EVENTS

Aus=Australia. B=Belgium. C.H.=Switzerland. E=Spain. F=France. G.B.=Great Britain. I = Italy. P = Portugal. R.A. = Argentina. S = Sweden. U.S. = United States of America.

43

Don't believe everything you read. Marquis de Portago came from Spain and not Portugal (P) as stated above. French-Brazilian Hernando Silva Ramos didn't come from Portugal either.

I only ever saw Juan Manuel Fangio aka 'El Chueco' ('the bandy-legged one') race once and that was in the 1956 British GP at Silverstone. I remember that his V8 Lancia-Ferrari sounded very loud! I also remember the cheering crowd as Hawthorn and Brooks in their BRMs took the lead at the start of the race. MT

Martin Tomlinson
'22

Chris Irwin

Chris Irwin was a rising talent who many considered could have been a Grand Prix winner after a stellar career in Formula 3. He showed speed in the 1967 Formula 1 season driving for Reg Parnell. For 1968 he signed to race in F2 for John Surtees and for Ford in the F3L sportscar. His season started well as he won the F2 Eifelrennen for Surtees on the Nürburgring South circuit. His next race was in the F3L on the Nordschliefe but in practice the car took off at the Flugplatz. His injuries were so severe that he never raced again. ARM.

The last entry in my autograph book

Raymond Mays

Raymond Mays from Bourne in Lincolnshire was a pre-war racing driver and earlier in his career was known for racing and winning in ERAs at venues as diverse as the Nürburgring, the Shelsey Walsh hillclimb and the Brighton Speed Trials which he dominated in the late 1940s. An engineer and entrepreneur Mays was one of the principals behind both ERA before WW2 and BRM after the War. The workshops of both firms were established in premises behind his family home. ARM

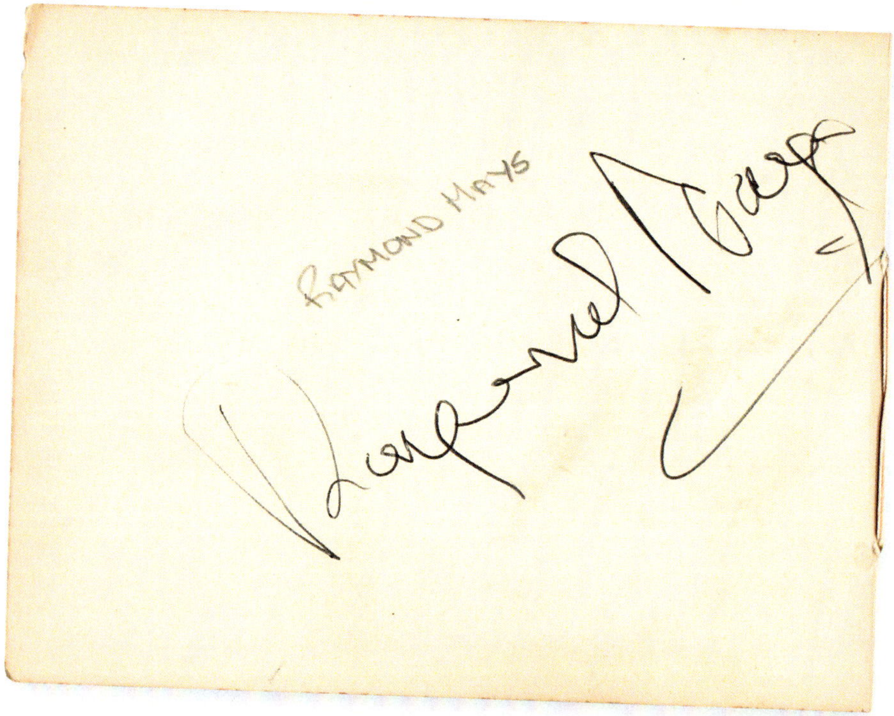

Raymond Mays, ERA, FTD Shelsey Walsh hill climb, 1936

Denis Jenkinson

Known as either DSJ – the initials under which he wrote in Motor Sport magazine - or just Jenks, he is considered to be the finest ever motor racing writer. But he tasted competition success too – as sidecar passenger to Eric Oliver he won 1949 World Sidecar Championship. In 1955 he navigated for Stirling Moss in his famous Mille Miglia win for Mercedes-Benz. ARM

'Toulo' de Graffenried, Alfa Romeo 158, Swiss GP, 1951

Tommy Wisdom

Tommy had a varied career both as a racer and as the Motoring Correspondent for the Daily Herald. He was a class winner in the Mille Miglia on three occasions and at Le Mans twice. He raced and rallied for a number of British car manufacturers such as Jowett, Bristol, Aston Martin and Jaguar. ARM

King Carl XVI Gustaf of Sweden

King Carl was the heir apparent to the Swedish throne when he signed Martin's book at Silveratone. He is a car enthusiast and owns several Porsche 911s, an AC Cobra, a Ferrari 456 and a vintage Volvo PV544. His son Prince Carl Philip races in the Porsche Carrera Cup Scandinavia and historic events. ARM

Emanuel 'Toulo' de Graffenried

Baron Emmanuel "Toulo" de Greffenreid was an aristocratic Swiss racer and one of the starters in the first World Championship race – the 1950 British GP. He raced privateer Maseratis and for the Alfa Romeo team and won the 1949 British GP at Silverstone. Later he was a consultant to Marlboro. ARM

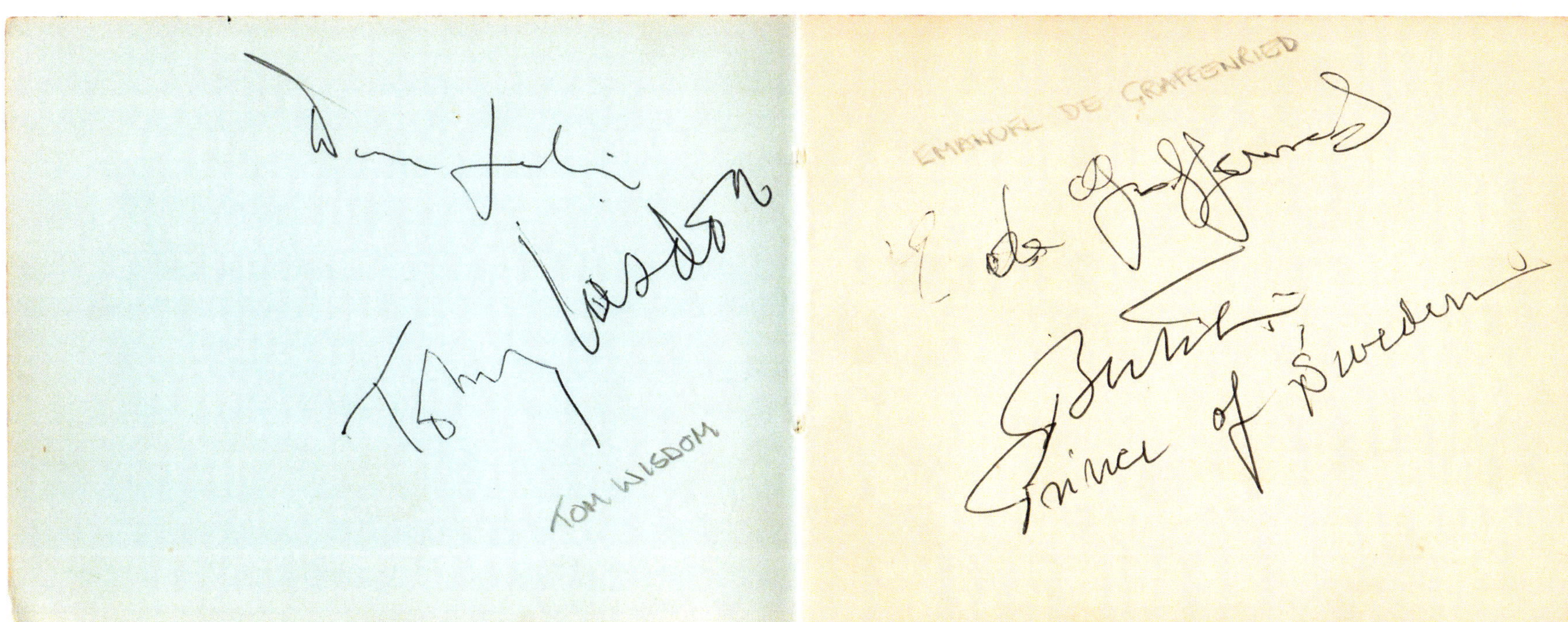

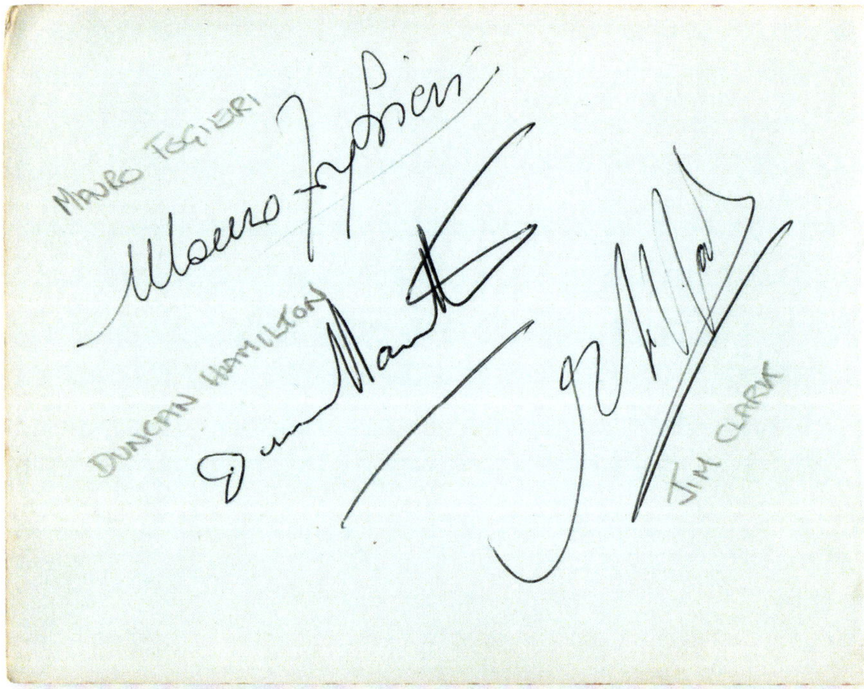

Mauro Forghieri

Mauro Forghieri was instrumental in many of Ferrari's greatest successes including World Championships in 1960s and 70s for John Surtees, Niki Lauda and Jody Scheckter. He took over the role of chief engineer of the Scuderia at the age of 27 when most of the senior team members left to unsuccessfully form a Ferrari rival. As an engineer he was highly respected throughout Formula 1 and designed chassis, engines and gearboxes. He later joined Lamborghini and then set up his own design consultancy. He died in his native Modena in 2022 aged 87. ARM

The Last Time

The 1967 British GP was another win for Jim Clark, and his fifth British GP. I don't know how many times I saw Jim Clark race, but it was a lot. Little did I imagine on that warm July afternoon that this was to be the last time. MT

Jim Clark

A border farmer, Scotsman Jim Clark is still considered by many to be the finest racing driver of all time, his effortless and stylist speed often crushing the opposition. A close bond formed with Lotus' Colin Chapman led to World Championships in 1963 and 1965 as well as victory in the 1965 Indianapolis 500. Yet he was a versatile driver who raced and won in sportscars and saloons, particularly a Lotus Cortina.

Racing against his parent's wishes in a little DKW saloon his talent was soon recognised by mentor Ian Scott-Watson of the Border Reivers team and by 1958 he was regularly winning in their Jaguar D-type and Porsche. At the end of the season in a Lotus Elite he was narrowly beaten by Chapman in a similar car. Chapman was impressed by the quiet Scot and hired him to drive in Formula Junior the following year. Thus started a partnership which only ended when Clark crashed into the trees in a Formula 2 race at Hockenheim in 1968 due to a mechanical or tyre failure.

Clark had made his Grand Prix debut in the 1960 Dutch GP and his first win came two years later in 1962. The following year was perhaps his best in the pencil-slim Lotus 25-Climax winning seven of the ten races. ARM

Duncan Hamilton (with Major Tony Rolt), C Type Jaguar, winners of 1953 Le Mans,

Jim Clark's finest! Clark, Lotus 49 took the lead on lap 3 of the Italian GP at Monza on 10 September 1967. However, on lap 13 he had to pit to replace a punctured rear tyre. and was lapped by the leading group. But by lap 21 he had un-lapped himself and went after the leaders Brabham and Surtees (Honda), who he passed into the lead on lap 60. On the last lap though, Clark's engine started cutting out with fuel feed problems and 'Black Jack' and 'Il Grande Giovanni' swept past and carried on racing to the flag where the latter won by 0.2 secs. Clark's Lotus, popping and banging, crossed the finishing in third place 23 seconds later. MT

SHELL
SHELL
SHELL
20
TEAM LOTUS
20
16
14
LOTUS

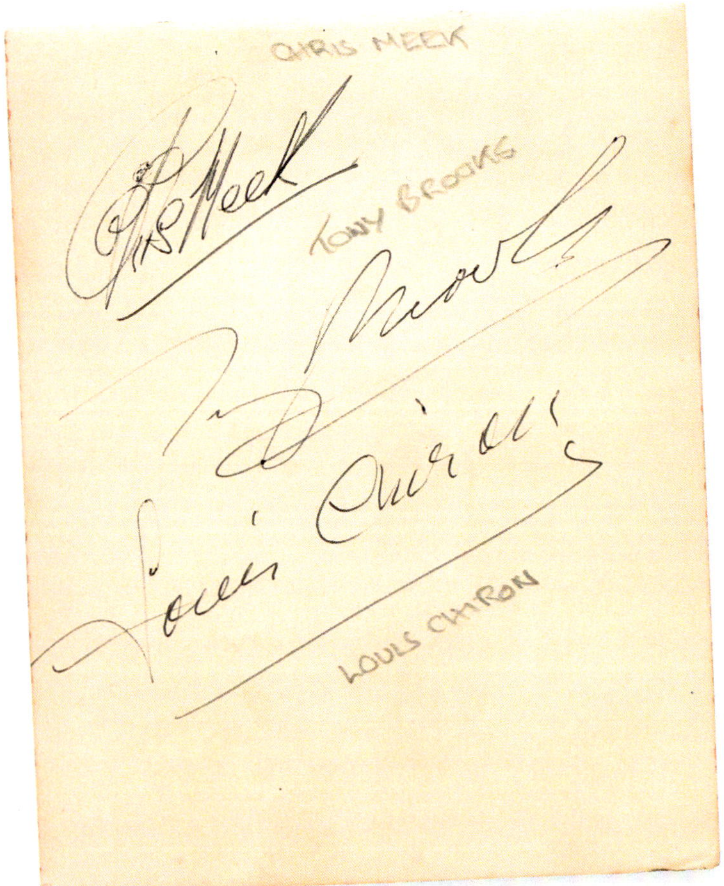

Chris Meek

Chris Meek's rich life embraced successful property development in Yorkshire, a long a and effective racing career which started in 500cc F3, later in Formula Ford, Formula Atlantic and sportscars which included everything from an Elva Courier to a Lotus Europa. He won the Production Sportscar series six times in the 1970s. He also sponsored rising talents such as Tom Pryce. He led a flamboyant life-style, and was said to have owned some 40 Ferraris over the years. For many years he was the owner of the Mallory Park race circuit. ARM

Tony Brooks

Known as the "racing dentist" Tony scored the first win by a British driver in a British car in a Formula 1 race since 1923. The race was the non-Championship Syracuse GP in 1955 when he was still a dental student. Hugely talented, he only competed in 39 Grands Prix and won six of them, racing for top teams such as Vanwall, Ferrari and BRM. One famous victory was at the British GP at Aintree, actually handing the Vanwall over to Stirling Moss in the later stages. Born in Cheshire, he started racing with a Frazer Nash in club events from 1952 until 1955 when he got a surprise chance to race a Connaught Formula 1 car at Crystal Palace. He finished fourth which led to his race at Syracuse.

This urbane and religious man was a twice winner of the German GP - at the Nürburgring and at Avus. He also won at great tracks like Monza, Spa and Reims. He was third in the 1958 World Championship for Vanwall and second a year later for Ferrari. In. sportscars he won the 1957 Nürburgring 1000 Kms and the 1958 Tourist Trophy with Moss for Aston Martin. But a couple accidents, including one at Le Mans, brought the dangers into focus and he retired early and for many years ran successful motor dealerships. He died in 2022 at the age of 90, the last surviving Grand Prix winner from the 1950s. ARM

Louis Chiron

Louis Chiron had a stellar career which covered some thirty years. He is in the record books as the oldest man to start a Grand Prix when he took part in. the 1955 Monaco GP, appropriately at the age of 55 and finished sixth in a Lancia D50.

Chiron started racing in 1926 and success came quickly in both a Bugatti and an Alfa Romeo He became one of the top drivers between the Wars and won not only the 1931 Monaco GP but also the Belgian, German, Italian and Moroccan GPs. He won the Spanish race three time but surpassing that he won the French GP on no fewer than five occasions both before and after the WW2. He also competed in the Indianapolis 500 and drove a Delage to 7th place and was also a winner of the Spa 24Hrs and the Monte Carlo Rally. But all nine attempts at Le Mans finished in non-finishes.

Chiron controversially accused the "Bugatti Queen" Hèlle Nice of being a Nazi collaborator. Bugatti attached his name to one of their supercars. Chiron died aged 80. ARM

This is how Sir Stirling Moss descibed team mate Tony Brooks; "Brooks was a tremendous driver, the greatest - if he'll forgive me saying this - 'unknown' racing driver there's ever been."

Tony Brooks was always at home on the fast 'classic' circuits like Spa (pictured), Nurburgring and Monza and in 1958 driving for the Vanwall team, he won all three of them, two more races than that year's World Champion Mike Hawthorn did in that season. MT

20
4

CASTROL
6
12
12

Art for Art's Sake

Other than motor racing, another great life-long passion of mine has been my art. This has brought me in touch with some of the 'greats' of motor racing - Chris Amon, Bob Bondurant, Phil Hill, Stirling Moss, Roy Salvadori, Carroll Shelby and John Surtees when they signed my prints. MT

S C H 'Sammy' Davis, winner of the1927 Le Mans 24 Hours with Dr Benjafield in a 3 litre Bentley

S C H Davis

I also had the great fortune to get to know SCH 'Sammy' Davis who was not only one of the 'Bentley Boys' and winner of the 1927 Le Mans but also an artist. Sammy was nearly 90 when I first met him, but you wouldn't know it. He was bright and alert and had an amazing recall of his early life. I would sit for hours whilst he told me about the great characters he knew and raced against in the 1920's and 1930's.

Unbelievable now but I have been fortunate to have known a man who, nearly a century ago, was a riding mechanic with Count Zborowski in the 1924 French GP. Their opposition that day included the winner Giuseppe Campari, his team mate Antonio Ascari - Alberto's father of course, Sir Henry Seagrave, Pietro Bordino and Robert Benoist as well as pre-WW1 stars Felice Nazzaro, Jules Goux and Louis Wagner. MT

Sydney Charles Houghton Davis, often referred to as SCH or Sammy was a racing driver, journalist and graphic designer and an inspiration to Martin. He raced at Le Mans for Bentley amongst others and won the 24 Hours for them in 1927. ARM

Few drivers have jumped the start in a more outrageous manner than Louis Chiron did at the start of the 1934 French GP.

A classic photograph of the start at the Montlhéry Autodrome shows the pack leaving the line but with no sign of Chiron. From a third row starting position the Monégasque had beaten everybody including the photographer and the starter as he tore away in the lead which he held until the chequered flag. MT

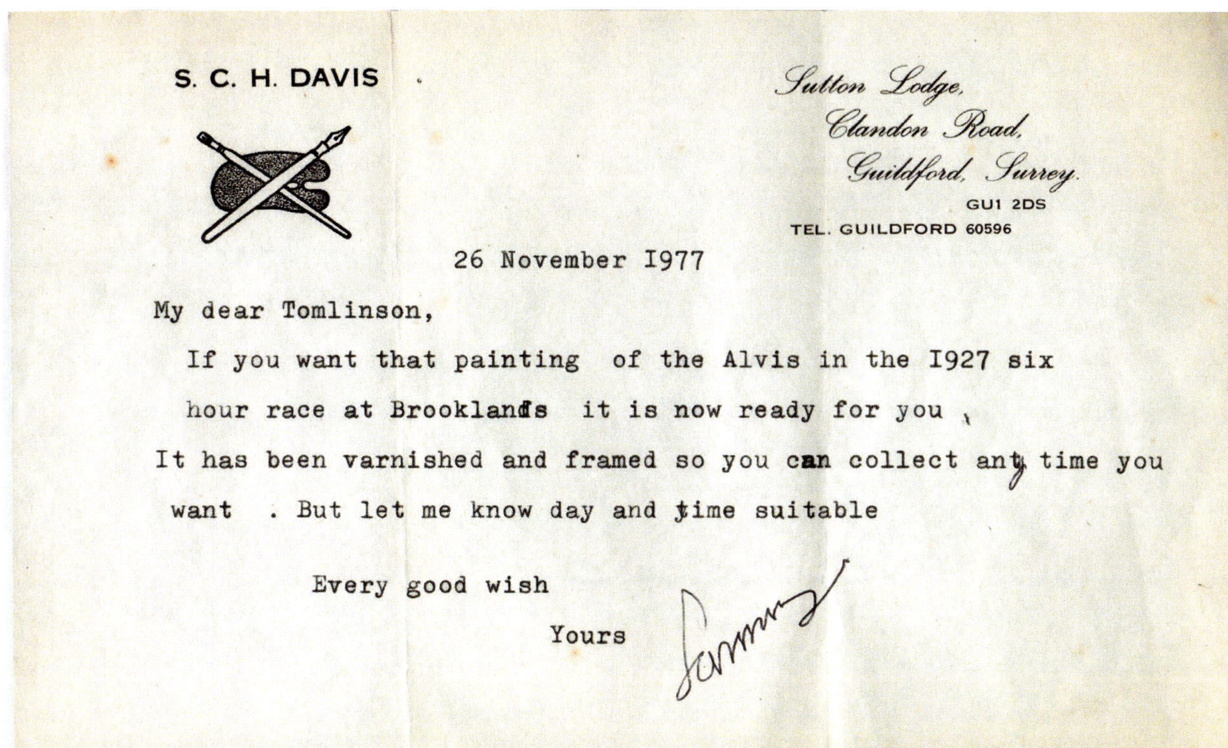

S. C. H. DAVIS

Sutton Lodge,
Clandon Road,
Guildford, Surrey.
GU1 2DS
TEL. GUILDFORD 60596

26 November 1977

My dear Tomlinson,

If you want that painting of the Alvis in the 1927 six hour race at Brooklands it is now ready for you. It has been varnished and framed so you can collect any time you want . But let me know day and time suitable

Every good wish

Yours

Sammy

Carroll Shelby signing prints in 1996 and his Le Mans winning co-driver Roy Salvadori doing the same at Goodwood House

John Surtees Limited
Monza House, Fircroft Way,
Edenbridge, Kent TN8 6EJ
Telephone: (01732) 865496 - 863773
Fax: (01732) 866945

Mr M Tomlinson
7 Kintbury
Duxford
Cambridgeshire
CB2 4RR

16 August 2000

Just a short note to express my appreciation of your kind thought in giving me the painting at Rye House. It was very much appreciated. Thank you.

Kind Regards

John Surtees

Director. J Surtees   Registered Office: 14-16 Station Road West, Oxted, Surrey RH8 9EP   VAT No. GB 367 3991 06
Registered In England No. 594362

With 'Il Grande Giovanni' ('Big John') and my painting of his Can Am winning Lola T70 at the Goodwood Festival of Speed

" I need to get some shut-eye.'

I can't remember now how the commission came about. But in 1996 I was asked by Chief Exec. of Addenbrooks Hospital, Cambridge to paint five works for the Carroll Shelby Foundation. Shelby had been receiving treatment for a heart condition at the hospital. Sales of prints of these paintings, signed by Shelby himself, would be a good way to raise money for the Foundation.

Then one day, out of the blue, I received a phone call from the Chief Exec. He asked me whether I had the time to take Carroll to the Coys Historic meeting at Silverstone where he was to attend the opening ceremony. He didn't have to ask twice!

By the time we arrived at the circuit Carroll was nearly asleep. He asked if I could go to the reception and pass on his apologies as he needed to get some "shut-eye" and could he sleep in my car for a while? I've never felt so important in my life when passing on his message to the good and great of the racing world!

An hour or so later a refreshed Carroll turned up at the art exhibition tent where I was exhibiting my work. From then on I spent the best part of the day with him. I listened to what the legend had to say on any number of different subjects, not all of which were motorsport related. It was a day that I will never forget. MT

Carroll Shelby

The Texan Carroll Shelby was a fine racing driver and Le Mans winner who went on to great success developing cars for the Ford Motor Company including the Mustang, the GT40 and the AC Cobra. From an early age he was fascinated with both cars and planes and he flew in the military with distinction. After WW2 he made a living as a chicken farmer. Amateur racing success in an MGTC and Cadillacs led to a professional career in 1959.

It was a meeting with the then Aston Martin racing boss John Wyer which vaulted him to International success. Shelby having impressed in a humble Cadillac at the Buenos Aires 1000 Kms. He became a regular in the team leading to such successes as his win Roy Salvadori in the 1959 Le Mans 24 Hours. He raced for Scuderia Centro Sud and Aston Martin in the 1958 and 1959 GPs seasons. He battled heart problems from an early age and later in life, the father of the Cobra, had a heart transplant in 1990. He died aged 89 in 2012. ARM

After ten years of trying, Aston Martin finally won the 'Grand Prix d'Endurance' at Le Mans in 1959. Carroll Shelby and Roy Salvadori drove the winning Aston Martin DBR1, finishing a lap ahead of their team mates Maurice Trintignant and Paul Frère. Shelby rushes through Maison Blanche in the early stages of the race. MT

5

Epilogue

How could I possibly better having Fangio's signature (twice!) in my autograph book? That was the main reason for me deciding not to carry on collecting autographs. I got a few more signatures later on the same day as Fangio's, but that was it!

Well, not quite. In July 1993 Maurice and I went to the Coys Historic Festival at Silverstone. As we wandered around the paddock we came across a long wooden bench, where in a row, sat Messrs Walker, Salvadori, Taylor, Redman and Brabham, signing autographs.

I suddenly thought that it would be a good idea to ask the group sat at the table to sign our programme which I could take home as a souvenir for my son Sam who wasn't with us that day. So I approached the group and asked if they wouldn't mind signing the programme cover. To which one of the assembled, I can't now remember which one, suggested in a jocular way "You're a bit too old to be asking us for autographs aren't you?" I replied, much to their combined amusement "They're not for me, they're for my son. I got all your autographs 30 odd years ago, but I'd like to have them in joined up writing this time please!" They all obliged. MT

Rob Walker

Rob Walker was an heir to the Johnny Walker whisky company but his passion was motor racing first, before the WW2, as a very handy driver and after it as the most successful Formula I privateer with drivers such as Stirling Moss, Graham Hill and Jo Siffert. Later he wrote eloquently for the US Road and Track magazine. ARM

Brian Redman

The Lancastrian Brian Redman raced on occasion for some of the best Formula I teams including Cooper and McLaren – he was third for Cooper in the 1968 Spanish GP – but he was far better known as one of the leading exponents of both Formula 5000 and Sportscar Racing.

He started racing in 1959 at the airfield track of Rufforth, near York in a Morris Minor, then a Mini. He graduated with help from mentor John Bridges of Red Rose Motors to a Jaguar E-type and a Lola T70 in which he had great success. Bridges also ran him in Formula 2.

He later won most of the major endurance races for the likes of Ferrari, Porsche, Alfa Romeo and Gulf, but success at Le Mans always eluded him and the closest he came was fifth overall. But he won the Spa 1000Kms four times and also scored victories in the Targa Florio, the Watkins Glen 6 Hours, Sebring 12 Hours, Daytona 24 Hours and the Monza 1000 Kms.

In the Formula 5000 category driving the big US V8-engined Lolas for Carl Haas and Jim Hall he triumphed in the US Championship in 1974, 1975 and 1976. There was also success in Can-Am. His career was punctuated by a couple of serious accidents. Based now in Florida, he is involved with running vintage car events and still competes occasionally. ARM

Brian Redman, who with Jo 'Seppi' Siffert won the Targa Florio in 1970 driving a Porsche 908. This is Redman rushing through the streets of the Sicilian town of Collesano.

It is one of my regrets that I never went to the Targa whilst it was still being run. To stand that close to the road whilst cars driven by the best drivers of the day hurtle past at racing speeds must have been quite something to behold! MT

12

It runs in the family

Sam with Froilan 'The Pamps Bull' Gonzales ...

... and with Jack Brabham as John Cooper signs his autograph book

END OF TEXT